Religion of the Heart

Religion of the Heart

Hannah More

Edited and mildly modernized by

Hal M. Helms

PARACLETE PRESS
Orleans, Massachusetts

First Printing, May, 1993

© 1993 by The Community of Jesus, Inc.
ISBN: 1-55725-063-4
Library of Congress #: 93-84600
Published by Paraclete Press
Printed in the United States of America

Table of Contents

Editor's Introduction

Who is Hannah More? Anticipating that this question might arise, we have included a brief biographical sketch of this remarkable woman who lived through one of the most interesting periods of history. The first answer to the question is, She is someone who has something useful and encouraging to say to us. "Being dead, she yet speaketh," to paraphrase the book of Hebrews.

This book was first published in 1811, and its title was "Practical Piety." Her object was to relate faith to living in a practical way. We knew that the language of almost 200 years ago would need some updating if we were to communicate with this generation. There have been many changes in writing styles and in word meanings since this book was written. At times we felt almost as though we were translating from a foreign language, and were astounded at our dearth of knowledge of things Hannah More takes for granted in her readers: knowledge of Shakespeare, poets, ancient history and foreign languages, Need to for instance. Her way of alluding to these things without be English being specific made our work more difficult but nonetheless intriguing. Sometimes her sentences were so constructed that the meaning was hard to decipher. Then, suddenly, the truth would break through in pithy, strong and unforgettable words. Our challenge has been to let this saint of God speak to our generation without losing her own voice.

Several colleagues have played a vital role in the preparation of this work. To them I offer my heartfelt thanks: Martin Shannon, Ronald Minor, William Showalter, Shelton Johnson and William Dubocq. Fr. Arthur Lane, Martha Conklin and Gertrude Andersen did the work of proof reading, as did my wife, Helen, who always encouraged us to "make it understandable." My thanks, too, to Paraclete Press, for asking for a new addition to the Living Library Series.

Echoing the sentiments of Hannah More, I would add that if this new edition helps people to think seriously about their commitment to our Lord and Savior, Jesus Christ, and to make theirs "a religion of the heart," our efforts will have been more than amply repaid.

Hannah More

(1745-1833)

Born in 1745 in a village about four miles from Bristol, England, Hannah More was the daughter of a local schoolmaster and one of five sisters. They were all said to be "pious, intelligent and highly competent," but Hannah was the most outstanding. From her father she gained her life-long interest in literature, and her early writings brought her into contact with London's literary circle. Dr. Samuel Johnson (of dictionary fame) was the leading figure of that fashionable group, and in spite of his usual bluntness, he called her "the most powerful versificatrix in the English language."

Although Hannah was attractive and enjoyed the company of men, she never married. At the age of twenty-eight, she received a proposal of marriage from an older man, Edward Turner, who lived a few miles south of Bristol. Apparently the thought of marriage was frightening to him, and after postponing the wedding date several times, actually left Hannah waiting at the church, only to call off the wedding with an apology. Without her knowledge, Hannah's longtime friend and neighbor, the Rev. Dr.

James Stonehouse, arranged for Turner to settle an annuity of two hundred pounds a year on her, enough to enable her to live comfortably.

Early in her life she met a number of luminaries in London society. Sir Joshua Reynolds and his sister became close friends. Others included Edmund Burke, the local Member of Parliament. Dr. Johnson and his good friend, David Garrick, were among the closest relationships formed in those years. Garrick was perhaps the foremost actor on the London stage, and did much to raise the reputation of actors in the eyes of society. Hannah became an avid admirer, and is reported to have seen him act twenty-seven times in one season. It was during this time that she first read a book by John Newton, the converted slave trader who was now rector of a London church. They soon became friends, and Newton served as her spiritual advisor. Newton was greatly responsible for Hannah's increasing concern with the African slave trade, an interest she also shared with her friend William Wilberforce, who spent most of his public life working for its abolition. David Garrick died in 1779, and after his death, Hannah continued to spend part of the winter months with his widow, Eva.

 Although she was now a successful poet and dramatist (several of her plays having been produced on the London stage), Hannah became increasingly uncomfortable with the social scene. She had always been devout, and Dr. Stonehouse, a dedicated evangelical, had helped form many of her lasting convictions on spiritual subjects. Finally she decided to abandon the London scene in favor of retirement to a country home, Cowslip Green, not far from Bristol. She writes with great openness about her continuing struggle with the desire for fame, and her growing conviction that this was inconsistent with her faith. Her "retirement" was soon interrupted by a series of visitors—"nobility, bishops, poets and a host of others all made Cowslip Green a place of pilgrimage."[1]

Her chronic asthma and bronchitis forced her to abandon her little thatched cottage in the winter. She took the occasion to visit a number of friends, according to the custom of the time, making the home of Eva Garrick her London headquarters. She also admits freely that her love of friends was a motivating factor in these yearly rounds. Whenever she could, she turned the conversation to spiritual things. A letter quoted in the Collingwood biography gives an insight into her concern for those whose lives were being wasted in the low level of society.

> "Miss _____ has also been with me several times—beautiful and accomplished; surrounded with flatterers and sunk in dissipation. I asked her why she continued to live so much below, not only her principles, but her understanding; . . . . did it make her happy? Happy, she said, no; she was miserable. She despised the society she lived in, and had no enjoyment of the pleasures in which her life was consumed; but what could she do? She could not be singular— she must do as her acquaintance did. I pushed it so home on her conscience, that she wept bitterly, and embraced me. I conjured her to read the Bible, with which she is utterly unacquainted. These fine creatures are, I hope, sincere, when they promise to be better; but the very next temptation that comes across them puts all their good intentions to flight and they go on, as if they had never formed them; nay, all the worse for having formed and not realized them. They shall have my prayers, which are the most effectual part of our endeavours."[2]

---

[1] Collingwood, Jeremy and Margaret, *Hannah More,* pp. 57, 58.

[2] Taken from Lady Chatterton, *Memorials of Admiral Gambier,* and quoted in Collingwood, pp. 60, 61.

In the late 1780's she became deeply involved in the efforts to abolish the slave trade. Together with John Newton, William Wilberforce, and the small group known as the Clapham Sect, she continued to write and agitate for reform. Her writings were very widely read and played no small part in rallying public support for that vicious and inhuman practice. After repeated defeats, the reformers were able to witness the abolition of the slave trade in Britain in 1807, and the complete abolition of slavery in 1833.

The story of Hannah's life moves on through her philanthropic attempts to help individuals who were in great need. Wilberforce awakened her interest in the appalling spiritual and moral conditions of the people of Somerset, and as a result, Hannah and her sisters began to set up Sunday schools and weekday schools in that area. Their object was to teach people to read, to train them in basic Christian truth, and to encourage them to live on a higher moral standard. She is credited with having helped "lay the foundation" for what we know as Victorian morality in England. The story of her success in such places as Cheddar, Nailsea and Shipham (all in Somerset, a few miles from her rural home) make fascinating reading.

Throughout the latter years of her life she was busy with her philanthropic concerns, her spiritual writings, and the succession of people who came to her for advice and counsel. Although she always suffered frequent bouts of illness, and although she spent much time in bed during her latter years, she outlived her four sisters by more than a decade. The chapter on the suffering Christian was written out of her own experience, and demonstrates the frame of heart in which she met the difficulties of her life. Her faith was summed up in these words: "I take my stand upon these two texts: *Without faith it is impossible to please God,* and *Without holiness, no man shall see the Lord."*

Charlotte M. Yonge says of her, "She had the honor

of making English ladies the foremost agents in the religious education of the poor. At first a writer of plays and poems which were the fashion of the Eighteenth Century, she afterwards devoted her talents to the lighter forms of religious literature for the masses, and again was a pioneer. Lastly, she wrote treatises on education, morals and religion which had great effect on her own generation."[3]

A recent biographical account says, "Instead of quiet domesticity, in obscurity, Hannah was to blaze a trail for women. By her own pen she earned a fortune, using it to set up a cottage industry producing moral tracts that sold in their millions in Britain, America and other parts of the English-speaking world. Through her pioneer work in the schools in the Mendip Hills near Bristol, she set in motion a whole new programme of popular education, and gave literacy and dignity to thousands of poor children. . . . It made no difference to her whether her pupils were the scruffiest and poorest children of Mendip miners or the leaders of society. To each she gave herself without reserve. Hannah became one of the major driving forces in teaching the nation to read." [4]

Editor's Note:

We were delighted to find that an interesting account of Hannah More's life had been published in England in 1990 by Jeremy Collingwood, vicar of Hotwells, and his wife Margaret, a freelance writer for BBC. Hannah More lived at Hotwells until her death. The book is published by Lion Publishing Corporation.

---

[3] Yonge, Charlotte M., *Hannah More.* (Eminent Women Series), W. H. Allen Co., 1888.

[4] Collingwood, *op. cit.,* pp. 7 and 8.

Chapter 1

Christianity: A Religion of the Heart

Christianity bears all the marks of its divine origin. It came down from heaven and its gracious purpose is to carry us up thither. Its Author is God. It was foretold from the beginning by prophesies which grew clearer and brighter as they approached the period of their accomplishment. It was confirmed by miracles which continued until the faith they illustrated was established. It was ratified by the blood of its Author. Its doctrines are pure, sublime, consistent; its precepts, just and holy. Its worship is spiritual. Its service is reasonable and is rendered practicable by the offers of divine aid to human weakness. It is accompanied by the promise of eternal happiness to the faithful and the threat of everlasting misery to the disobedient. It had no collusion with power, for power sought to crush it. It could not be in any league with the world, for it set out by declaring itself the enemy of the world: it condemned the world's maxims, it showed the vanity of its glories, the dangers of its riches and the

1

emptiness of its pleasures.

Christianity, though the most perfect rule of life that was ever devised, is far from being merely a rule of life. A religion consisting of a mere code of laws might have sufficed for mankind in a state of innocence, but those who have broken these laws cannot be saved by a rule which they have violated. What consolation could we find in the perusal of statutes, every one of which brings a fresh conviction of our guilt and fresh assurance of our condemnation? The chief object of the Gospel is not to furnish rules for the preservation of innocence, but to hold out the means of salvation to the guilty. It does not rest on suppositions, but on facts; not upon what might have suited us in our state of original purity, but upon what is suitable to us in the urgency of our fallen state.

The Christian faith does not consist of an external conformity to practices which, though right in themselves, may be adopted from human motives to serve unworthy purposes. It is not a religion of forms, modes and decencies. True Christianity means being transformed into the image of God. It means becoming like-minded with Christ. It considers Him as our sanctification as well as our redemption. It endeavors to live *to* Him here that we may live *with* Him hereafter. It means desiring earnestly to surrender our will to His, our heart to the leading of His Spirit and our lives to the guidance of His Word.

The Scriptures declare that a change in the human heart is necessary, and they picture it to be not so much an old principle improved as a new one created. Christians are not educated out of their former character, but are given a new one. This change is expressed in great varieties of language and under different figures of speech. Since it is so frequently described in almost every part of the Sacred Writings, this doctrine of the necessity of change of heart should be held in reverence. Instead, it is sometimes mocked in obnoxious terms.

The Scriptures frequently point out the comparison between natural and spiritual things. The same Spirit which moved upon the face of the waters in the creation of the world operates on the human character to produce a new heart and a new life. By this operation, the affections and faculties of the person receive a new impulse: our dark understanding is illuminated, our rebellious will is subdued, our irregular desires are rectified. Our judgment becomes informed, our imagination is chastised, our inclinations are sanctified, our hopes and fears are directed to their true and proper end. Heaven becomes the object of our hopes, an eternal separation from God becomes the object of our fears. Our love of the world is transformed into the love of God. Our senses have a higher direction. The whole internal frame and constitution receive a nobler bent; the intents and purposes of the mind are given a more sublime aim; our aspirations gain a loftier flight, our vacillating desires find a fixed object; our wandering purposes find a settled home; *and* our disappointed heart finds a sure and certain refuge. Instead of worshipping the world, that heart now struggles to become the world's conqueror. Our blessed Redeemer, in overcoming the world, bequeathed us His command to overcome it also. And He did not give the command without the offer of power to obey the command.

Genuine religious faith demands not merely an external profession of our allegiance to God, but an inward devotedness to His service. It puts the Christian into a new state of things, a new condition of being. It raises us above the world even while we live in it. It disperses the illusions of sense by opening our eyes to realities instead of those shadows we had been pursuing. Our faith shows this world as a scene whose original beauty has been darkened and disordered by sin, and it shows humankind as helpless and dependent creatures. It points to Jesus Christ as the repairer of all the evils which sin has caused and as our restorer to holiness and happiness. Any religion short of this is not that faith which the Gospel has presented to us. It is not the faith which our Redeemer came down to earth to teach us, to illustrate by His example, to confirm by His death, and to consummate by His resurrection.

Christianity does not always produce these happy effects to the full extent I have expressed, but it always has a tendency to produce them. If we do not see its effects to be such as the Gospel attributes to the transforming power of true faith, it is not because of any defect in the principle, but to the remains of sin in the heart, to the imperfectly subdued corruptions of the Christian. Those who are very sincere are still very imperfect. They evidence their sincerity by acknowledging the inadequacy of their attainments and by lamenting what remains of their corruptions. Many an humble Christian whom the world reproaches with being overzealous, whom it ridicules for being enthusiastic in his aims and rigid in his practice, is inwardly mourning for the opposite reason. He would bear their criticism more cheerfully if he did not feel his danger to lie in the opposite direction. He is secretly abasing himself before his Maker for not carrying far enough the very principle which the world accuses him of carrying too far. The fault which others find in him is excess. The fault he finds in himself is deficiency. He is, alas! too commonly right. His enemies speak of him as they hear. He judges of himself as he feels. But, though humbled to the dust by the deep sense of his own unworthiness, he is "strong in the Lord and in the power of His might." "He has," says the venerable Hooker, "a Shepherd full of kindness, full of care, and full of power." His prayer is not for reward but for pardon. His plea is not merit but mercy; but then it is mercy made sure to him by the promise of the Almighty to penitent believers.

The mistake of many in their religious life appears to be that they do not begin with the beginning. They do not lay their foundation in the conviction that humanity is by nature in a state of alienation from God. They consider mankind as an imperfect rather than as a fallen creature. They allow that we need to be improved but deny that we need a thorough renovation of heart.

Genuine Christianity, however, can never be grafted on any other stock. The design to reinstate beings who have not fallen, to propose a restoration without a previous loss, a cure where there was no radical disease, is altogether an incongruity which would seem too obvious to require confutation if we did not so frequently see the delusion being expressed. Would there be "deliverance to the captive" if there had been no captivity? Would the Lord proclaim "the opening of the prison to them that are bound," if there had been no prison, no bondage? (Luke 4:18)

We are aware that many consider the doctrine in question as a bold charge against our Creator. But may we not venture to ask, Is it not a bolder charge against His goodness to presume that He had made beings originally wicked, and against God's truthfulness to believe that, having made such beings, He pronounced them "good"? Is not that doctrine more reasonable which is expressed or implied in every part of Scripture, that the moral corruption of our first parents has been passed on to all their posterity, and that from this corruption (though only punishable for the actual offenses) they are no more exempt than from physical death?

We must not, however, think falsely of our nature. We must humble but not degrade it. Our original brightness is obscured but not extinguished. If we consider ourselves in our natural state, our estimation cannot be too low;

when we reflect at what a price we have been bought, we can hardly overrate ourselves.

If, indeed, the Almighty had left us to the consequence of our natural state, we might have rebelled against His justice with more show of reason. But when we see how graciously He has turned our very lapse into an occasion of improving our condition, to advance us to a greater good than we had lost, how God has raised us to a higher condition than that which we forfeited, to a happiness greater than that from which we fell, this gives us an impression of the immeasurable wisdom and goodness of God and of the unsearchable riches of Christ.

The faith about which we are speaking has sometimes been misunderstood and often misrepresented. It has been described as an unprofitable theory, and has been ridiculed as a fanciful extravagance. For the sake of distinction we call it "the religion of the heart." It dwells in the heart as the fountain of spiritual life, and from there it sends forth an abundance of life and warmth through the whole personality. There, in the heart, is the soul of virtue, the vital motivation which moves the whole being of a Christian.

This faith has been the support and consolation of the sincere believer in all ages of the Church. That it has been perverted both by the cloistered and the un-cloistered mystic, not merely to promote abstraction of mind, but inactivity of life, makes nothing against the faith itself. What doctrine of the New Testament has not been made to speak the language of its thoughtless advocate, and turned into arms against some other doctrine which it was never meant to oppose?

But if it has been carried to a blameable excess by the pious error of holy persons, it has also been adopted by the less innocent fanatic and used for the most pernicious purposes. The extravagance of the fanatic has furnished arguments to the enemies of internal religion, which they use against the sound and sober exercise of genuine faith. They seize every occasion to represent it as if it were criminal, as the foe of morality. They regard it as the proof of unsound minds, mischievous, hostile to active virtue and destructive to public usefulness.

But if these charges are really well founded, then the brightest luminaries of the Christian Church— Chrysostom, Augustine, the Reformers and the Fathers, the goodly fellowship of the prophets, the noble army of martyrs, the glorious company of the apostles, then Jesus Himself (I shudder at the implication!)—were all baseless conjecturers, fanatic enthusiasts, enemies of virtue and subverters of the public good.

Those who disbelieve or reject this inward faith are to be greatly pitied. Their belief that no such principle exists will, it is to be feared, keep it from existing in themselves. Not being sensible to the needs of their own hearts, they establish this as a proof of its impossibility in all cases. This persuasion, as long as they maintain it, will assuredly prevent them from receiving divine truth. What they assert can be true in no case, cannot be true in their own. Their hearts will be barred against any influence of the power which they do not believe exists. They will not desire it, they will not pray for it, except in the Liturgy, *where it is the prescribed language.*[1] They will not accustom themselves to those exercises to which that language invites them, exercises which the Church loves and cherishes. Thus they expect the end, but avoid the way that leads to it. They affirm the hope of glory, while they neglect or pervert the means of grace. But let not the formal religionist who has probably never sought, and therefore, never obtained, any sense of the spiritual mercies of God, conclude that there is no such state. His

---

[1] She obviously refers to the "unbelieving church-goer"—in a time when church-going was an expected part of being an Englishman.

lack of understanding of it is no more proof that no such state exists than the cheering pleasures of a genial climate prove that such a climate does not exist.

Where our own hearts and experience do not illustrate these truths practically so as to afford us some evidence of their reality, let us examine our minds and faithfully follow up our convictions. Let us enquire whether there has really been a failure in the accomplishment of God's promises, or whether we have been sadly deficient in yielding to those suggestions of conscience which are the motions of His Spirit. Let us ask whether we have not neglected to implore the aid of that Spirit; whether we have not, in too many instances, resisted His nudges. Let us ask ourselves if we have looked up to our heavenly Father with humble desire. Having repeatedly implored His direction, do we endeavor to submit ourselves to its guidance? Having prayed that His will may be done, do we ever stoutly set up our own will in contradiction to His?

If, then, we do not receive the promised support and comfort, the failure must rest somewhere. It lies between Him who has promised and those to whom the promise is made. There is no other alternative. Would it not be blasphemy to transfer the failure to God? Let us not, then, rest until we have cleared up the difficulty. The spirits sink and faith fails, if, after a continued round of reading a prayer, after having conformed to the letter of the command for years, after having scrupulously brought in our quota of outward duties, we find ourselves just where we were at setting out.

We complain justly of our own weakness, and truly plead our inability as a reason why we cannot serve God as we ought. This weakness, its nature and its measure, God knows far better than we know it; yet He knows that, with the help which He offers us, we can both love and obey Him, or He never would have made it the qualification of our obtaining His favor. He never would have said, "Give me thy heart"—"Seek ye My face"—"Add to your faith virtue"—"Have a right heart and a right spirit"—"Strengthen the things that remain"—if all these precepts did not have a definite meaning and if they had not been *practicable* duties. (Prov. 23:26; Ps. 27:8; II Peter 1:5; Ps. 51:10; Rev. 3:2)

Can we suppose that the omniscient God would have given these unqualified commands to powerless, incapable beings who could not be persuaded? Can we suppose that He would paralyze His creatures and then condemn them for not being able to move? He knows, it is true, our natural impotence, but He also bestows a divinely induced strength. There is scarcely a command in the whole of Scripture which has not either immediately or in some other part, a corresponding prayer and a corresponding promise. If it says in one place, "Get yourselves a new heart," it says in another, "A new heart will I *give* thee," and in still another, "*Create* in me a clean heart!" (Ezek. 18:31; 36:26; Ps. 51:10) It is worth observing that a diligent enquirer may trace everywhere this threefold union. If God commands by St Paul, "Let not sin reign in your mortal body," (Rom. 6:12) He promises by the same Apostle, "Sin shall *not* have dominion over you." (Rom. 6:14) Then, to complete the threefold agreement, He made David *pray* that his sins may not have dominion over him.

The saints of old, so far from setting up on the foundation of their own independent virtue, seem to have had no idea of any light except what was imparted, of any strength but what was given them from above. Their urgent petitions run, "O send forth Thy light and Thy truth!" (Ps. 43:3) Their grateful assurances declare, "The Lord is my strength and my salvation!" (Ps. 118:14) And their praise is expressed thus: "Bless the Lord, O my soul,

at is within me bless His holy name." (Ps. 103:1)
ugh we must be careful not to mistake for the
agency those impulses which pretend to operate
independently of external revelation and have little
reference to it, the internal witness is that powerful agency
which sanctifies all outward means and renders all external
revelation effectual. All the truths of our faith, all doctrines
of salvation are contained in the Holy Scriptures, but these
very Scriptures require the influence of that Spirit which
inspired them to produce an effective faith. The Holy Spirit,
by enlightening the mind, converts the rational thinking
and brings the intellectual conviction of divine truth
contained in the New Testament into an operative
principle. Thus by reading, examining and enquiring, we
may reach such a reasonable assurance of the truth of
revelation as to remove all doubts from our mind. But
this mere intellectual faith alone will not operate against
our corrupt affections, it will not cure our besetting sins,
will not conquer our rebellious wills. A mere historical
faith and the most reasonable evidence of its truth are
not substitutes for heart religion.

An habitual reference to the Spirit which animates the
real Christian strengthens the truth of revelation but never
contradicts it. The Word of God is always in unison with
His Spirit. His Spirit is never in opposition to His Word.
We are aware that we are treading on dangerous ground
because it is disputed ground. Among the fashionable
curtailments of Scriptural doctrines, there is not one truth
which has been lopped from the modern creed with a
more unsparing hand than this one. There is not one
which excites more suspicion toward those who advocate
it. But if it is a mere phantom, should we with such careful
repetition have been warned against neglecting or
opposing it? If the Holy Spirit could not be "grieved,"
might not be "quenched," were not likely to be "resisted,"
that very Spirit who proclaimed the prohibitions would

never have said, "Grieve not," "Quench not," "Resist not." The Bible never warns us against imaginary evils nor holds out imaginary goods. If then, we refuse to yield to the Spirit's directions, if we do not submit to His gentle persuasions and if we reject His directions, (for such they are, and not arbitrary compulsions) we shall never attain to that peace and liberty which are the privilege and the promised reward of sincere Christians.

In speaking of that peace which passeth understanding, we do not allude to those illuminations and raptures which God may have in some instances bestowed, but which He has nowhere promised to bestow. We refer rather to that hope which flows from an assurance of the paternal love of our heavenly Father. We speak of that life and power of faith which are the privilege of those "who abide under the shadow of the Almighty," (Ps. 91:1) of those who know in whom they have believed, of those "who walk not after the flesh but after the Spirit," (Rom. 8:4) of those who endure "as seeing Him who is invisible." (Heb. 11:27)

Many faults may be committed where there is nevertheless a sincere desire to please God. Many weaknesses still exist along with a cordial love of our Redeemer. Faith may be sincere where it is not strong. But they who can conscientiously say that they seek the favor of God above every earthly good, that they delight in His service more than in any other gratification, that to obey Him here and to enjoy His presence hereafter is the prevailing desire of their heart and that their chief sorrow is that they do not love Him more nor serve Him better—such persons require no evidence that their heart is changed and their sins forgiven.

The happiness of a Christian does not consist in mere feelings which may deceive, nor in moods which may be only occasional. Rather, it consists in a settled, calm conviction that God and eternal things have the predominance in our heart. It consists in a clear perception that eternal concerns have, though with much weakness, the supreme, if not undisturbable, possession of our minds. Our chief remaining sorrow is that we do not surrender ourselves to our convictions with as complete yieldedness as we ought. These abatements, though sufficient to keep us humble, are not powerful enough to make us unhappy.

The true measure to be taken of our state is from a perceptible change in our desires, tastes and pleasures; from a sense of progress, however small, in holiness of heart and life. This seems to be the safest rule of judging, for if mere feelings were allowed to be the criterion, the presumptuous would be inflated with spiritual pride from the enjoyment of them, while the humble, from their very humility, might be just as unreasonably depressed because they lack such feelings.

The recognition of this divine aid of the Spirit then, involves no presumption, raises no illusion, causes no inflation of the ego. It is both sober and rational. In establishing the law of God it does not reverse the law of nature, for it leaves us in full possession of those natural faculties, while it improves and sanctifies them. So far from inflaming the imagination, its tendency is to subdue and regulate it.

A security which outruns our attainments is a most dangerous state, yet it is a state some Christians unwisely covet. The probable way to be safe hereafter is not to be presumptuous now. If God graciously grants us inward consolation, it is only to animate us to further progress. It is given to us for support in our way, not to settle us in our present condition. If the promises are our food, the commandments are our work. Temperate Christians ought to desire nourishment only in order to carry us through our business. If we rest passively on the promises so as to grow sensual and indolent, we might become both unwilling and incapable of performing our work. We must not expect to live upon tonics which only serve to inflame without strengthening. Even without an over-reliance on these promises, which we are more ready to desire than to put ourselves in the way to obtain, there is an inward peace in a humble trust in God and in a simple reliance on His Word. There is a repose of spirit, a freedom from worry in the lowly confidence in Him, for which the world has nothing to give in exchange.

On the whole, then, the state we have been describing is not the dream of the enthusiast. It is not the reverie of the visionary who renounces duties for fanciful speculations and who embraces shadows as reality. Rather, it is that sober promise of Heaven, that reasonable anticipation of eternal happiness which God is graciously pleased to grant to *all* who diligently seek His face, to *all* to whom His service is freedom, His will is law, His Word a delight, His Spirit a guide. That blessed anticipation is given to all who love Him sincerely and devote themselves to Him, saying "Lift up the light of Thy countenance upon us, O Lord!" (Ps. 4:6)

Chapter 2

Christianity: A Practical Faith

If God is the Author of our spiritual life, then the best evidence we can give that we have received something of this life is an unreserved dedication to the promotion of His glory. We ought not to flatter ourselves that we are in the favor of God if our life is not consecrated to the service of God. The only unequivocal proof of such a consecration is that we are more zealous of good works than those who do not even pretend to be controlled by any such motive.

The finest theory never carried anyone to heaven. A religion of opinions which occupies the mind without filling the heart may obstruct our salvation but can never advance it. If these opinions are false, they are most pernicious. If true and not operative, they aggravate guilt. If they are unimportant though not sinful, they occupy a place which belongs to nobler objects and sink the mind below its proper level. Such a religion is not that which Christ came to teach mankind. All the doctrines of the

Bible are practical principles. The Word of God was not written, the Son of God was not incarnate, the Spirit of God was not given only that Christians might obtain right views and possess correct ideas. True faith is something more than correctness of opinions, rightness of conceptions and exactness of judgment. It is a life-giving principle. It must be infused into the habit as well as enlightening the understanding. It must regulate the will as well as directing the creed. It must not only cast the opinions into a new frame, but the heart into a new mold. It changes the tastes, gives strength to the new inclinations, and together with a new heart, produces a new life.

Christianity urges the same temper, the same spirit, the same dispositions on all who profess it. Specific acts or the outward expression of our faith must depend on circumstances which do not depend on us. The power of doing good is withheld from many from whom the reward will not be withheld. If the external act constituted the whole value of Christian virtue, then the Author of all good would be Himself the Author of injustice, by putting it out of the power of multitudes to fulfill His own commands. In motives, attitudes, in fervent desires and in holy efforts are found the very essence of Christian duty.

We must not fondly attach ourselves to the practice of some particular virtue, or set our value exclusively on some favorite quality. Nor must we wrap ourselves up in the performance of some particular action as if it formed the sum of Christian duty. But we must embrace the whole law of God in all its aspects and relations. We must bring no fancies, no partialities, no prejudices into our religious duties, but take them as we find them and obey them as they are shown in the Bible without addition, curtailment or contamination.

We must not condemn a person for a single really bad action nor praise him for a single apparently good one. If so, Peter's denial would render him the object of our condemnation, while we should have judged favorably the prudence of Judas. Who does not know the catastrophe of Judas? Peter, on the other hand, became a glorious martyr to that Master whom, in a moment of weakness, he had denied.

A religious faith which is thoroughly spiritual and disconnected from all outward circumstances was not made for such a complex and imperfect creature as man. There have indeed, been a few sublime spirits, not "touch'd but rapt," who seem almost to have literally soared above this earthly terrain. They appear almost to have stolen the fire from the Seraphim and to have had no business on earth but to keep alive the celestial flame. They would, however, have imitated more nearly the example of their divine Master if they had combined a more diligent discharge of the active duties and beneficent deeds with their high devotional attainments.

But while we are in little danger of imitating them, let us not censure the devout error of these exalted spirits too harshly. Their number is small. Their example is not catching. Their ethereal fire is not likely to inflame the world. The world will take due care not to come in contact with it while their distant light and warmth may accidentally cast a useful ray on the cold-hearted and the worldly.

But from this small number of refined beings, we do not intend to draw our notions of practical spirituality. God did not make a religion for these few exceptions to the general state of the world, but for the world at large. He made it for active beings, busy, restless persons whose activity He diverts into its proper channels by His Word, directing our busy spirits to the common good. Since our restlessness indicates the unsatisfactoriness of all we find on earth, He points us to a higher destination. If total seclusion and abstraction had been designed to be the general state of the world, God would have given us other laws, other rules, other faculties, and other employments.

There is a class of visionary but godly writers who seem to shoot as far beyond the mark as mere moralists fall short of it. People of low views and gross minds may be said to be wise *below* what is written in God's law, while others whose refinement is almost too subtle, are wise *above* it. The first group grovels in the dust from the deadness of their intellectual faculties, while the others are lost in the clouds by stretching their minds beyond their appointed limits. The one builds spiritual castles in the air instead of erecting them on the holy ground of Scripture. The other group lays its foundation in the sand instead of resting it on the Rock of Ages. Thus the superstructure of both is equally unsound.

God is the fountain from which all the streams of goodness flow. He is the center from which all the rays of blessedness shine. All our actions are, therefore, only good insofar as they have a reference to Him: the streams must revert to their Fountain, the rays must converge again to their Center.

If love for God is the governing principle, this powerful spring will actuate all the movements of the reasonable creature. The essence of religious faith does not so much consist in actions as in affections. Though right actions may be performed where there are no right affections, they are a mere carcass, utterly devoid of soul, and therefore, of virtue. On the other hand, genuine affections cannot substantially and truly exist without producing right actions. Let it never be forgotten that a devout inclination which does not have life and vigor enough to ripen into action when the occasion presents itself has no place in the account of real goodness. Neither can right actions without sound underlying principles have any place. A good inclination will be contrary to sin, but an inclination alone will not subdue sin.

Since the love of God is the source of every right

direction and feeling, it is the only principle which necessarily involves the love of our fellow-creatures. As man we do not love man. There is a love of partiality but not of benevolence; of friends and favorites, but not of humanity collectively. It is true we may, and do, without this principle, relieve human distress, but we do not bear with human faults. We may promote human well-being, but we do not forgive offenses. Above all, we are not anxious for the immortal interests of our fellow man. We could not see them in need without feeling pain, but we can see them in sin without emotion. We could not hear of a beggar perishing at our door without feeling horror, but we can witness an acquaintance dying without repentance and feel no concern. Is it not strange that we must partake somewhat of the divine nature before we can really love the human? It seems indeed to be our insensibility to sin rather than our lack of benevolence toward mankind that makes us naturally pity their temporal conditions and be careless of their spiritual poverty. But does not this very insensibility proceed from lack of love for God?

As true virtue consists in the habitual frame of mind, occasional good actions are no certain criteria of the state of the heart. Who is there who does not occasionally do them? But we must not sit down, having made a little progress, feeling satisfied that we have inclinations to virtuous actions but fail to carry them through. If our Christian commitment is a true one, it will never be passive and inert. We shall never do good with any great effect till we labor to be conformed in some measure to the image of God, and we shall best show evidence of having obtained something of that conformity by steady and active obedience to God.

Every individual should bear in mind that we are sent

into this world to act a part in it. Though one may have a more splendid task, while another has a more obscure part assigned to him, yet each is equally accountable. Though God is not a hard Master, He is an exact one. He accurately proportions His requirements to His gifts. If He does not expect that one talent should be as productive as five, yet to even a single talent He annexes a proportional responsibility.

He who has said, "Give me thy heart," (Prov. 23:26) will not be satisfied with less; He will not accept the praying lips nor the mere gesture of charity as substitutes.

A real Christian will be more just, more sober and charitable than others, though he will not rest for salvation on justice, sobriety or charity. He will perform the duties they require in the spirit of Christianity as instances of devout obedience, as evidences of a heart devoted to God.

All virtues, it cannot be repeated too often, are sanctified or unhallowed according to what motivates them. They will be accepted or rejected accordingly. This motivation, kept in due exercise, becomes a habit, and every act strengthens the inclination, adding strength to the motive and pleasure to the performance.

We cannot be said to be real Christians until faith becomes our governing motive, our predominating guide and pursuit, just as worldly things are the predominating guide and pursuit of worldly souls.

New converts, it is said, are most zealous, but they are not always the most persevering. If their tempers are warm and they have only been touched on the side of their feelings, they start eagerly, march rapidly and are full of confidence in their own strength. They too often judge others with little charity and themselves with little humility. They think that those who move steadily are standing still, and they fancy their own course will never be slackened. If their conversion has not been solid, when religion loses its novelty it will lose its power. Their speed declines.

Indeed, it will be fortunate if their motion does not go into reverse. Those who are truly sincere will usually be persevering. If their speed is less eager, it is more steady. As they come to know their own heart more fully, they discover its deceitfulness and learn to distrust themselves. As they become more humble in spirit they become more charitable in judgment. As they grow more firm in principle they grow more careful in their conduct.

The rooted habits of a religious life may indeed lose their prominence because they have become more deeply ingrained. If they are not embossed, it is because they are indelibly burned in. Where there is uniformity and consistency in the whole character, there will be little outward show in specific actions. A good deed will be less striking in an established Christian than a deed less good in one who had been previously careless. Good actions are the expected duty and ordinary practice of the Christian. Such a Christian indeed, when his right habits cease to be new and striking, may fear that he is declining, but his quiet and confirmed course is a surer evidence than the initial starts of charity or fits of religious zeal which may have drawn more attention and gained more applause.

We should cultivate most assiduously, because the work is most difficult, those graces which are most opposite to our natural dispositions. The value of our good qualities depends very much on their being produced by the victory over some natural wrong propensity in us. The implantation of a virtue is the eradication of a vice. It will cost one person more to keep down a rising passion than to do a brilliant deed. It will test another more to keep back a sparkling but corrupt thought which his wit had suggested, but which his conscience checks, than it would to give a large sum to charity. Godly souls are deeply sensible of the worthlessness of any actions which do not spring from the genuine fountain, and they will aim at such a habitual conformity to the divine image that to perform all acts of justice, charity, kindness, temperance and every related virtue, may become the habitual and abiding state of their heart, so that like natural streams they may flow spontaneously from the living source.

Practical Christianity then, is the active operation of Christian principles. It means keeping watch for occasions to exemplify those principles. It is "exercising ourselves unto godliness." (I Tim. 4:7) We cannot tell in the morning what opportunities we may have of doing good during the day; but if we are sincere, we will try to keep our hearts open, our minds prepared and our affections alive to do whatever may occur in the way of duty. We will, as it were, stand in the way to receive the orders of Providence. Doing good is our vocation. We reject no duty that comes within the sphere of our calling, nor do we think the work we are employed in a good one if we might be doing a better one. Having done a good action well simply furnishes us with a new reason for embarking on the next one. We look not at the work we have accomplished, but on that which we have yet to do. Our views are always prospective. Our charities may be limited by our power, but our wills know no limits. Our fortune may have bounds, but our benevolence has none. We are, in mind and desire, benefactors of everyone in misery. Our hearts are open to all the distressed, and when it comes to the household of faith, they overflow. Where the heart is large, however small the ability, a thousand ways of doing good will be invented. Christian charity is a great enlarger of means. If Christian self-denial cannot fill the purse by a wish, it will not empty it by a vanity. It provides for others by self-denial. Having carefully defined what is necessary and fitting, it allows no encroachment on its definition. It will trim and cut off excesses and vanities. The deviser of liberal things will find ways of effecting them, which appear incredible to the indolent, and to the covetous they will seem impossible. Christian beneficence takes a large sweep. That circumference cannot be small of which God is the center. Nor does religious charity in a Christian stand still because it is not kept in motion by the mainspring of the world. Money may fail, but benevolence will be going on. If we cannot relieve want and need, we may mitigate sorrow. We may warn the inexperienced, we may instruct the ignorant, we may confirm the doubting. Christians will find out the cheapest way of *being* good as well as of *doing* good.

If we cannot give money, we may exercise a more difficult virtue: we may forgive injuries. Forgiveness is the economy of the heart. Christians will find it cheaper to pardon than to resent. Forgiveness saves the expense of anger, the cost of hatred, the waste of spirits. It also puts the soul into a frame which makes the practice of other virtues easy. The achievement of a hard duty is a great abolisher of difficulties. If great occasions do not arise, we can thankfully seize on small ones. If we cannot glorify God by serving others, we know that we always have something to do at home, some evil temper to correct, some wrong inclinations to reform, some crooked practice to straighten. We can never be at a loss for employment while there is a sin or a misery in the world. We will never be idle while there is a distress to be relieved in another or a corruption to be cured in our own hearts. We have employments assigned to us for every circumstance in life. When we are alone, we have our thoughts to watch; in the family, our tempers; when in company, our tongues.

What an example of disinterested goodness and unbounded kindness have we in our heavenly Father, who is merciful over all His works! He distributes common blessings without distinction, bestows the necessary refreshments of life, the shining sun and the refreshing shower, without waiting (as we are apt to do) for personal merit or gratitude. God does not look to see who are the deserving ones, but who are the needy ones. He does not afflict willingly but delights in the happiness of all His children and desires their salvation. Daily He dispenses generously, daily He bears with our offenses. In return for our violation of His laws, He supplies our necessities, patiently waits for our repentance, and even urges us to have mercy on our own souls!

What a model for our humble imitation is that divine Person who was clothed with our humanity! He dwelt among us so that the pattern might be rendered more engaging and conformity to it made more practicable. His life was one of unbroken, universal charity. He never forgot that we are compounded both of soul and body, and after teaching the multitude, He fed them. He repulsed none for being ignorant, was impatient with none for being dull, despised none for being loathed by the world, and He rejected none for being sinners. Our Lord encouraged those whose forgiveness others criticized; in healing sicknesses He converted souls; He gave bread and forgave injuries.

Christians must seek to express their morning devotions in their actions through the day. We must try to make our conduct a practical expression of the divine prayer which has been made part of them. We will desire to hallow the name of God, to promote the enlargement and the coming of the Kingdom of Christ. We will endeavor to do and allow God's whole will, to forgive as we trust to have been forgiven. We will resolve to avoid that temptation into which we have prayed not to be led, and will seek to shun the evil from which we have asked to be delivered. We make our prayers as practical as the other parts of our religious faith, and labor to render our conduct as spiritual as our prayers.

If our gracious Savior has left us a perfect model for

our devotion in His prayer, He has left a model no less perfect for our practice in His Sermon on the Mount. This divine exposition has been sometimes misunderstood. It was not so much a supplement to a defective law, as the restoration of the purity of a perfect law from the corrupt interpretations of its imperfect expounders. These interpreters had ceased to consider it as forbidding the sinful motive, but only the sinful act. Christ restored it to its original meaning, spread it out in its due extent, showed the largeness of its dimensions and the spirit behind it. Not contenting Himself, as human legislators are obliged to do, to prohibit a man the act which brings injury to others, He addressed the inward disposition behind the act.

There cannot be a more striking instance of the way every doctrine of the Gospel has reference to practical goodness than is exhibited by St Paul in that magnificent picture of the resurrection in his epistle to the Corinthians. The Church has selected this Scripture for the consolation of those who have lost loved ones in death. After an inference as triumphant as it is logical, that because "Christ is risen we shall also rise," Paul compares the raising of the body from the dust to the process of grain sown in the earth and springing up into a new mode of existence. Then he goes on to describe the subjugation of all things to the Redeemer, sketching with a seraph's pen the relative glories of the celestial and terrestrial bodies, and after all this, the apostle winds up drawing an unexpectedly practical conclusion: "*Therefore,* my beloved, be ye steadfast, unmovable, always abounding in the work of the Lord." Then at once, by another quick transition, he resorts from the duty to the reward, concluding with an argument as powerful as his language had been sublime, adding, "Forasmuch as you know that your labor is not in vain in the Lord." (I Cor. 15:58)

Chapter 3
Mistakes in Religion

To point out all the mistakes which exist today on the awesome subject of religion would far exceed the limits of this small work. No mention therefore is intended to be made of the opinions or the practice of any particular body of people, nor will any notice be taken of any of the peculiarities of the numerous sects and parties which have risen up among us. It will be sufficient to remark on a few of those characteristics which belong to most groups of Christians.

There are among many others, three different sorts of professed Christians. One sort consists in a sturdy defence of what they themselves call orthodoxy, an attendance on public worship and a general decency of behavior. They are quite apprehensive of excess, not understanding that their own danger lies in the other direction. Although they are far from rejecting faith and morals, they are somewhat afraid of *believing* too much and a little scrupulous about *doing* too much, lest they be suspected of fanaticism. These Christians consider religion as a point they have obtained by their regular observances, which requires nothing else but to maintain it by repeating the same observances. They are satisfied to remain where they are, considering that they have obtained their goal and, of course, are saved the labor of further pursuit. They are to keep their ground without troubling themselves in search of some imaginary perfection.

These frugal Christians are most afraid of excess in their optional duties. They are apt to weigh in the nicely-poised scales of scrupulous exactness the duties which must of hard necessity be done, and those which without risk can be left undone. They give up through fear a trivial gratification to which they are less inclined, and snatch doubtingly at another which they like better. The gratification in both cases might be something hardly worth contending for, even if spiritual considerations were out of the question. Nothing but love to God can conquer love of the world. One grain of that divine motivation would tilt the scale of self-indulgence.

These persons dread enthusiasm more than anything else. Yet if enthusiasm causes one to look for effects without their predisposing causes, to depend for Heaven on something for which Heaven was never promised—if such be features of enthusiasm—then they themselves are enthusiasts.

The religion of the second group has been described in the two earlier chapters. It consists in a heart devoted to its Maker, one that is inwardly changed in temper and disposition, yet deeply sensible of its remaining infirmities. Continually aspiring to higher improvements in faith, hope and charity, they believe that *charity* is the greatest of these. These Christians are regarded as enthusiasts by the former class, but they are in fact acting on the *only* rational principles. If the doctrines of the Gospel have any solidity, if its promises have any meaning, these Christians are building on no false ground. They hope that submission to the power of God, obedience to His laws, compliance with His will, trust in His Word, are through the operation of the Eternal Spirit, real evidences of their genuine faith in Jesus Christ. Although they profess not to place their reliance on works, they are nevertheless more zealous in performing them than the others who profess to depend on their good deeds for salvation but are not always diligent to secure it by the very means they declare to be essential.

There is a third class—"the high flown Christian" who looks down from the giddy heights of antinomian delusion on the other two, abhors the one and despises the other, and concludes that one is lost and the other is almost so.[1] Though perhaps they are not in immorality themselves, they do not hesitate to imply in their words that virtue is heathenish and good works unnecessary if not dangerous. They do not consider that, though the Gospel promises that God "remembers our sins no more," (Jer. 31:34) it nowhere promises pardon to those who continue to live in a state of rebellion against God and of disobedience to His laws. They forget to insist to others that it is of little importance even to believe that sin is an evil while they continue living in it; that to know everything about duty except the doing of it is to offend God with an aggravation from which only ignorance itself is exempt. It is not giving ourselves up to Christ in some nameless, inexplicable way which will avail us. God loves a humble, not an audacious faith. To suppose that the blood of Christ redeems us from sin while sin continues to pollute the soul is to suppose an impossibility. To maintain that it is effectual for salvation, but not for the sanctification of the sinner, is to suppose that it acts like an incantation, an amulet which is to produce its effect by operation on the imagination but not on the disease.

The faith which mixes with human passions and is set on fire by them will temporarily make a stronger blaze

---

[1] Antinomians held that under the Gospel the moral law is of no use or obligation and that faith alone is necessary for salvation.

than that light which is from above which sheds a steady and lasting brightness on the path and communicates a sober but durable warmth to the heart. The light from above is equable and constant, while the human light, like a cooking fire fed by coarse materials, is extinguished all the sooner by its intensity.

That religion which is merely seated in the feelings is not only liable to wear itself out by its own impetuosity, but is apt to be driven out by some other passion. The feelings crowd one another out, "dispossess" one another, as it were. When such faith has had its day, it gives way to the next usurper. Its empire is no more solid than it is lasting when the motive and reason do not fix it on the throne of the heart.

The first of the above groups considers prudence as the paramount virtue in religion. Their diametrical opposites, the "super-spiritual" group believes a burning zeal to be the exclusive grace. *They* reverse St Paul's discussion of the three Christian graces and think that the greatest of these is *faith*. Though even in respect of this grace, their conduct and conversation too often give us reason to lament that they do not bear in mind the genuine and distinctive features of faith. Their faith seems to be adopted from a notion that the Christian has nothing to do, rather than the fact that it is faith's nature to lead us to do more and better than others.

In this case, as in many others, that which is directly contrary to what is wrong, is also wrong. If each opponent would only barter half his favorite quality with the favorite quality of the other, both parties would come nearer to the truth. They might even furnish a complete Christian between them, provided the zeal of the one was sincere and the prudence of the other was honest! But the misfortune is that each is as proud of *not* possessing the quality he lacks, because his adversary has it, as he is proud of possessing that which the other lacks.

Among the many mistakes in religion, it is commonly thought that there is something so unintelligible, absurd and fanatical in the term "conversion," that those who employ it run no small hazard of being ridiculed. It is seldom used but ludicrously or in contempt. This arises partly from flippancy and ignorance, but perhaps as much, too, from the imprudence and enthusiasm of those who have absurdly confined it to real or supposed instances of sudden or miraculous changes from dissipation to godliness. But surely with reasonable people we run no risk in asserting that some are awakened by various methods the Almighty uses to bring His creatures to the knowledge of Himself. Seeing the corruptions that are in the world and feeling those with which their own hearts abound, these souls are brought, some gradually, some more rapidly, from an evil heart of unbelief to a lively faith in the Redeemer. As they turn from a life of gross vice or simply one of worldliness and vanity, to a life of growing holiness, they are surely as sincerely converted by the same divine power as if some instantaneous revolution had taken place in their character. The doctrines of Scripture are the same now as when David called them "a law *converting* the soul, and giving *light* to the eyes." (Ps. 19:7,8) This is perhaps the most accurate and comprehensive definition of the change for which we are contending, for it includes both the illumination of the understanding and the alteration of the heart.

If then this unpopular expression signifies nothing more or less than that change of character which consists in turning from the world to God, however the *term* may offend, there is nothing ridiculous in the *thing*. Since it is not for the term we contend but for the principle conveyed by it, so it is the principle and not the term which is the real ground of objection. Many who would sneer at the idea of conversion would be offended if it were suspected that their own hearts were not turned to God.

Reformation is a term against which no objection is ever made. If words continued to retain their original meaning, it would convey the same idea as conversion. For it is plain that to *re-form* means to make anew. In present usage, however, it does not convey the same meaning. Many people are reformed on human motives, many are partially reformed; but only those who are "reformed altogether" are converted. No complete reformation in the conduct is effected without a revolution in the heart. To cease from some sins while retaining others in a lesser degree, or to adopt such sins as are merely respectable, or to exchange one sin for another, or to cease from the external act without any internal change of heart, these are not examples of Christian reformation. The new principle must abolish the old habit. The rooted inclination must be conquered by the substitution of an opposite one. The natural bias must be changed. The actual offence will no more be pardoned than cured if the inward corruption is not eradicated. To be "alive unto God through Jesus Christ" must follow "the death unto sin." (Rom. 6:11) There cannot be new aims and ends where there is not a new principle to produce them. We shall not choose a new path until a light from Heaven directs our choice and guides our feet. We shall not "run the way of God's commandments" until God Himself enlarges our heart. (Ps. 119:32)

The change required does not preclude the possibility of falling into sin, but it is a change which fixes in the soul such a disposition as shall make sin a burden and the desire to please God the governing desire of our heart. It will make the paltriness of our attainments the source of our deepest sorrow. A Christian has hopes and fears as well as other men. God in changing the heart does not extinguish the passions. Were that the case, the Christian life would cease to be a warfare.

We are often deceived by that partial improvement

which appears in the victory over some bad habit or attitude. But we must not mistake the removal of a symptom for a radical cure of the disease. An occasional remedy might remove an accidental sickness, but it requires a general regimen to renovate the diseased constitution.

It is the natural but sad history of the unchanged heart that, from youth to advanced years, the only revolution in the character actually increases both the number and quality of its defects: the levity, vanity and self-sufficiency of the young man is carried into advanced life, to meet and mix with the defects of old age. Instead of crying out with the royal prophet, "O remember not my old sins," (Ps. 79:8) the unchanged is stirring up the memories of them by new ones. Age, prolonging all the faults of youth, furnishes its own contingent of vices, so that sloth, suspicion and covetousness swell the account which a vital faith has not been called in to cancel. Although the world has lost the power to delight, it has lost nothing of its power to enslave.

Instead of improving in honesty by the inward sense of its own defects, that very consciousness makes such a person less tolerant of the defects of others and more suspicious of their apparent virtues. His charity in former years failed to bring him that return of gratitude for which it was partly reformed. Having never flowed from the genuine spring, it is now dried up. Since friendships were formed from worldly motives, ambition or sociable enjoyment, they now fail him. "One must make some sacrifices to the world," is the prevailing language of the nominal Christian. "What will the world pay you for your sacrifices?" we ask. Though that nominal Christian finds that the world is insolvent, that it pays nothing of what is promised (for it cannot bestow what it does not possess, viz. happiness), yet such a one continues to cling to it almost as confidently as if it had never disappointed him. If we were called on to name the condition which excites the deepest sadness in the heart, which contains the sum and substance of real human misery, we should not hesitate to say AN IRRELIGIOUS OLD AGE. The debility of declining years, even in the godly person, though they evoke sympathy, yet it is the sympathy of tenderness without distress. We take and give comfort from the cheering persuasion that the exhausted body will soon cease to weigh down its immortal companion, the soul, and that dim and failing eyes will soon open on a world of glory.

Dare we paint the reverse picture? Dare we allow the imagination to dwell on the opening prospects of the ungodly elder? Dare we figure to ourselves that the weakness, miseries and terrors we are now lamenting, are ease, peace and happiness compared with the unutterable prospect which lies ahead?

There is a fatal way of lulling the conscience by entertaining diminishing thoughts of sins long since committed. We persuade ourselves to forget them and we therefore persuade ourselves that they are not remembered by God. But though distance diminishes objects to the eye of the beholder, it does not actually lessen them. Their real size remains the same. Deliver us, merciful God, from the delusion of believing that secret sins, of which the world has no cognizance, early sins which the world has forgotten but which are known to "Him with whom we have to do," (Heb. 4:13) become by secrecy and distance as if they had never been! "Are not these things noted in *Thy* book?" (Ps. 56:8) Perhaps, if we remember them, God may forget them, especially if our remembrance be accompanied by a sound repentance. If we remember them not, He assuredly will. The holy contrition which should accompany this remembrance, while it will not lessen our humble trust in our compassionate Redeemer, will keep our conscience tender and our heart watchful.

We do not deny that there is frequently much kindness, benevolence and generosity in people who do not even pretend to be Christians. These qualities often flow from constitutional feeling, natural softness of temper and warm affections. Often they come from a good education, that best *human* sweetener and polisher of social life. We feel a tender regret as we exclaim, "what fine soil would such dispositions afford to plant religious faith in!" Well-bred persons are accustomed to respect all the decorums of society, to connect the ideas of personal comfort with public esteem, or generosity with credibility, or order with respectability. They have a keen sense of dishonor and are careful to avoid what may bring discredit on their name. Public opinion is the breath by which they live, the standard by which they act. Of course they would not lower by gross misconduct that standard on which their happiness depends. They have been taught to respect themselves; this they can do with more security while they retain the respect of others.

In some who make further advances towards true faith, it is dwarfish and stunted; it makes no shoots. Though it gives some signs of life, it does not grow. By a tame and spiritless routine, or rather by this fixed and immoveable position, they rob themselves of that fair reward of peace and joy which attends on a humble consciousness of progress. The feeling of difficulties and a sense of divine favor should be our experience. Faith which is profitable is usually observable. Nothing supports a traveler in his Christian course like the conviction that he is getting on. It is like looking back on a country we have passed, and above all, it is like the sense of that protection which has carried us hitherto and of that grace which has promised to support us to the end.

The proper direction of the renewed heart is upward. True religion is of an aspiring nature, continually tending towards that heaven from which it came. Its top is high because its root is deep. It is watered by a perennial fountain. In its most flourishing state it is always capable of further growth. Real goodness proves itself by a continual desire to be better. No virtue on earth is ever in a complete state. Whatever stage of spirituality one has attained, if we are satisfied to rest in that stage, we could not truly be called religious. The Gospel seems to consider the highest degree of goodness as the lowest with which a Christian ought to sit down satisfied. We cannot be said to be finished in any Christian grace, because there is not one which may not be carried further than we have carried it. This promotes the double purpose of keeping us humble as to our present state, and of stimulating us to something higher which we may hope to attain.

Superficial things are dignified by the term "religion" by people of the world, though they bring just that degree of credit which is a major motivation in worldly Christians. These things neither bring comfort for this world nor security for the next. Outward observances, indispensable as they are, are not religion. They are the accessory but not the principal. They are important aids and adjuncts, but not the thing itself. They are its nourishment but not its life, the fuel but not the fire, the scaffolding but not the building. Religious faith can no more subsist merely by them than it can subsist without them. They are divinely appointed and must be conscientiously observed, but observed as a means to promote an end, not as ends in themselves.

The robot-like adherence to formal worship where the living power does not give life to the form, the cold tribute of ceremonial attendance without the animating motive will neither bring peace to our own mind, nor will it satisfy a jealous God. That God whose eye is on the heart, "who trieth the reins and searcheth the spirits," (Ps. 7:9) will not be satisfied that we make Him little more than a nominal Deity while the world is the real object of our worship. Some seem to have almost the entirety of observance and lack only the soul of it. They are constant in their devotions, but the heart they keep away. They read the Scriptures, but rest in the letter instead of testing themselves by their spirit. They consider reading the Bible as an enjoined task, but they do not regard it as the quick and powerful instrument put into their hands for the critical dissection of "piercing and dividing asunder the soul and spirit." They do not regard the Scriptures as the penetrating "discerner of the thoughts and intents of the heart." (Heb. 4:12) These well-intentioned persons seem to spend a considerable portion of time in religious exercise, and yet complain that they make little progress. They almost seem to suggest that the Almighty did not keep His word with them, and show that their religious practice is not to them "pleasantness" and "peace."

To such we may ask, Would you not do better to examine than to complain? Should you enquire whether you do, indeed, possess a heart which is sincerely devoted to God, notwithstanding its imperfections? He who does not desire to be perfect is not sincere. Would you not do well to convince yourselves that God is faithful, that His promises do not fail, that His goodness is not slackened? May you not be entertaining some secret unfaithfulness, practicing some unconscious disobedience, withholding some part of your heart, neglecting to exercise your faith, subtracting something from your devotedness to which the promises of God are annexed? Do you indulge no preferences contrary to His will? Do you never resist the dictates of His Spirit, never shut your eyes to His illumination, nor your hearts to His influence? Do you not indulge some cherished sin which obscures the light of grace, some practice which obstructs the growth of virtue, some distrust which chills the warmth of love? The discovery will repay the search, and if you succeed in this scrutiny, let not the detection discourage, but stimulate you.

If you then resolve to take your faith in earnest,

especially if you have actually adopted its customary forms, do not rest in such paltry attainments as will afford neither present peace nor future happiness. To know Christianity only in its outward forms and its internal dissatisfactions, its superficial outer appearances and its disquieting apprehensions within, is a state of penalty rather than pleasure. It is the desire to stand well with the world as a Christian, yet to be unsupported by a well-founded Christian hope, to depend for happiness on the opinion of others instead of the favor of God. It is to go on dragging through the mere exercises of religious observances without deriving from them real strength or solid peace: to live in dread of being called an enthusiast by outwardly exceeding in religion but in secret consciousness of falling short of it, to be conformed to the world's view of Christianity, rather than to aspire to be transformed by the renewing of your mind. This is a state, not of conquest but of hopeless conflict, not of trusting love but of tormenting fear. It is knowing religion like a captive in a foreign land knows the country in which he is a prisoner. He hears from the cheerful natives of its beauties, but is himself ignorant of everything beyond his own gloomy limits. He hears that others are free and happy, but feels nothing himself but the harshness of incarceration.

Godly character is little understood by the devotees of the world. If it were, they would be struck with its grandeur. It is the very reverse of that meanness, cowardice and narrowness of view which they ascribe to it.

A Christian lives at the height of his being, not only at the top of his spiritual but of his intellectual life. Christians alone live in the full exercise of their rational powers. Religious faith ennobles the reason while it enlarges it.

Let your soul act up to its high destination instead of groveling in the dust. Do not live so much below itself. You wonder why you are not more stable, when you perpetually rely on things which are not stable themselves. In the rest of a Christian there is stability. Nothing can shake our confidence but sin. Outward attacks and trouble rather fix than unsettle us, as tempests from without only serve to root the oak more firmly. On the other hand, inward attacks will gradually rot and decay our confidence.

These are only a few of the mistakes among the multitude which might have been pointed out, but they are common and everyday occurrences. The ineffectiveness of such faith will be obvious.

That religion which reduces Christianity to a mere conformity to religious usages must always fall short of substantial effects. If sin is seated in the heart, that is the place where it must be fought. It is in vain to attack it in the suburbs when it is lodged in the center. Mere forms can never expel that enemy which they can never reach. A religion of decencies may drive our corruptions out of sight, but they will never drive them out of possession. If they are expelled from their outer edges, they will retreat to their citadel. If they do not appear in the grosser forms prohibited by the Ten Commandments, still they will exist. The shape may be altered but the principle will remain. He who dares not be revengeful will be unforgiving. He who ventures not to break the letter of the seventh commandment in act will violate it in spirit. He who has not courage to forfeit heaven by gross immorality will seek to scale it by pride or will lose it by unfruitfulness.

Our names are not written in the Book of Life by some vain hope built on external privileges or performance nor a presumptuous confidence. It is endeavoring to keep all the commandments of God, living to Him who died for us, being conformed to His image as well as redeemed by His blood. This is Christian virtue, this is the holiness of a believer. A lower motive will produce a lower morality, but God does not accept such an unsanctified morality.

It will avail us little that Christ has died for us, that

He has conquered sin, triumphed over the powers of darkness and overcome the world, while any sin retains its unresisted dominion in our hearts, while the world is our idol, and while our fostered corruptions cause us to prefer darkness to light. We must not persuade ourselves that we are reconciled to God while our rebellious hearts are not reconciled to goodness.

It is not casting a set of opinions into a mold and a set of duties into a system which constitutes the Christian faith. The circumference must have a center; the body must have a soul. The performances must have a motive. Outward observances were wisely constituted to rouse our forgetfulness, awaken our worldly spirits and call back our negligent hearts. But it was never intended that we should stop short in the use of them. They were designed to evoke holy thoughts, to quicken us to holy deeds, but not to be used as substitutes for either. Many find it cheaper, however, to serve God in a multitude of exterior acts than to starve one interior corruption.

Nothing short of that uniform stable principle, that fixedness in religion which directs us in all our actions, aims and pursuits to God as our ultimate end can give consistency to our conduct or tranquility to our soul. Once this state is attained, we will not waste all our thoughts and designs on the world. We will not lavish all our affections on so poor a thing as our own advancement. We will desire to devote all to the only object worthy of them, to God. Our Savior has taken care to provide that our ideas of glorifying Him may not run out into fanciful delusions or subtle inventions by simply stating: *"Herein is my Father glorified that you bear much fruit."* This He goes on to tell us is the true evidence of our being of the number of His people, by adding: *"So shall you be my disciples."* (John 15:8)

Chapter 4
Sporadic Spirituality

We greatly deceive ourselves when we think that what is called *the world* is only to be found in this or that situation. The world is everywhere. It is a nature as well as a place; a principle as well as a "local habitation and a name." Though the principle and the nature flourish most in those haunts which are their congenial soil, yet we are too ready, when we withdraw from the world to bring it home with us, to lodge it in our own bosom. The natural heart is both its temple and its worshipper.

But the most devoted idolater of the world, with all the capacity and industry which he may have applied to the subject, has never yet been able to accomplish the grand design of uniting the interests of heaven and earth. This experiment which has been more assiduously and more frequently tried than one can tell, has been singularly unsuccessful. The most laborious process seeking to reconcile the Christian faith with the world has never yet been competent to make opposing principles hang together.

But to drop a metaphor. Faith is never thoroughly

enjoyed by a heart full of the world. The world in return cannot be completely enjoyed where there is just faith enough to disturb its false peace. In such minds heaven and earth ruin each others' enjoyments.

There is a religious commitment which is too sincere for hypocrisy, but too sporadic to be profitable. It is too superficial to reach the heart, too unproductive to proceed from it. It is slight but not false. It has discernment enough to distinguish sin, but not firmness enough to oppose it. It has compunction enough to soften the heart, but not vigor sufficient to reform it. It laments when it does wrong, and performs all the functions of repentance of sin except forsaking it. It has everything of devotion except the stability, and gives everything to faith except the heart. This is a spirituality of times, events and circumstances. It is brought into play by situations and dwindles away with the occasion which called it out. Festivals and fasts which occur but seldom are much observed, and it is to be feared, *because* they occur but seldom. The great festival, the Lord's Day, which comes every week, comes too often to be so respectfully treated. The piety of these people is very visible in sickness, but is apt to retreat again as recovery approaches. If they die, they are spoken of by their admirers as though they are saints. If they recover, they go back into the world they had renounced and again suspend their amendment as often as death suspends its blow.

There is another class whose views are still worse. They cannot shake off religion enough to be easy without retaining its brief and stated forms, and they contrive to mix up these forms with a faith consistent with their practice. They blend their inconsistent works with a vague and unwarranted reliance on what the Savior has done for them, and thus patch up a merit and a propitiation of their own—running the hazard of incurring punishment by their lives, and inventing a scheme to avert it by their creed. Religion never interferes with their pleasures except by a short and occasional suspension. Having got through their occasional acts of devotion, they return to the same scenes of vanity and idleness which they had discontinued for the temporary duty. They forget that it was the very purpose of those acts of devotion to cure the vanity and to correct the idleness. Had the sporadic observance answered its true design, it would have made them averse to the pleasure instead of giving them a dispensation for its indulgence. Had they used the devout exercise in a right spirit, and employed it for its true purpose, it would have set the heart and life at work on all those pursuits which it was calculated to promote. But their project has more ingenuity. By the minutes they give to religious devotion, they purchase a protection at a cheap price for the misuse of the rest of their time. They make these periodical devotions a kind of spiritual insurance, which make up to the adventurers in pleasure any loss or damage which they may sustain in its voyage.

It is of these shallow devotions, these presumed equivalents for a new heart and a new life, that God declares by the prophet that He is "weary." (Isa. 1:14) Though of His own express appointment, the stated observances become "an abomination" to Him as soon as the sign comes to be substituted for the thing signified. We Christians have our new moons and our sacrifices under other names and other shapes, of which sacrifices (speaking of the spirit in which they are offered), the Almighty has said, "Bring no more vain oblations. . . ; the new moons and sabbaths, the calling of assemblies, I cannot endure them. They are iniquity." (Isa. 1:13).

We pray and solemnly pledge ourselves weekly in the General Confession, that we may "ever hereafter live a godly life, by giving up ourselves not only with our lips, but with our lives." Is this sporadic spirituality a fulfillment of that prayer? Is giving an hour or two to public worship on Sunday morning what it means to make the Sabbath "a delight"? Do we "honor the Sabbath day" by desecrating the rest of it in going our own way and finding our own pleasure?

Sometimes in a sermon, these sporadic religionists hear with awe and terror of the hour of death and the day of judgment. Their hearts are penetrated with the solemn sound. They acknowledge the awful realities by the impression made on their own feelings. The sermon ends, and with it the serious reflections which it excited. While they listen to these things, especially if the preacher is alarming, these thoughts are all in all to them. They return to the world, however, and these things are as if they had never been, as if their reality lasted only while they were being preached, as if truth were truth only when it attracted their notice. As soon as their minds are disengaged from the question, one would think that death and judgment were an invention, that heaven and hell were blotted from existence, that eternity ceased to be eternity in the long intervals in which eternal things cease to be the object of *their* consideration.

This is the natural effect of what we venture to call "sporadic spirituality." It is a passing homage kept totally distinct and separate from the rest of their lives, instead of making these religious observances the prelude and the principle of a life of devout practice. They do not weave their devotions and their actions into one uniform tissue by doing all in one spirit and to one end. When worshippers of this description pray for "a clean heart and a right spirit," when they beg of God to "turn away their eye as from beholding vanity," (Ps. 119:37) is it not to be feared that they pray to be made what they resolve never to become, that they would be very unwilling to become as good as they pray to be made, and would be sorry to be as penitent as they profess to desire? But alas!! They are in little danger of being taken at their word.

There is too much reason to fear their petitions will not be heard or answered, for prayer for the pardon of sin will obtain no pardon while we retain the sin in hope that the prayer will be accepted without the renunciation.

The most solemn office of our religion is the sacred Memorial of the death of our Lord, the blessed command and tender testimony of His dying love. Holy Communion is the consolation of the humble believer, the gracious appointment for strengthening our faith, quickening our repentance, awakening our gratitude and kindling our charity. It is too often resorted to, however, on the same erroneous principle. Those who venture to live without the use of this Holy Communion live in a state of disobedience to the last request of our Redeemer. Those who rest in it as a means for taking the place of constant commitment to Him totally mistake its design and are fatally deceiving their own souls.

It is to be hoped that this Sacrament is rarely attended, even by this class of Christians, without a desire to approach it with the devout feelings described above. But if they carry them to the altar, are they equally anxious to carry them away from it, are they anxious to maintain them afterward? Does the Sacrament so seriously approached leave for them any vestige of seriousness behind it? Are they careful to perpetuate the feelings they were so desirous to excite? Do they strive to make them produce solid and substantial effects? Would that this inconstancy of mind were to be found only in this class of characters under consideration! Let us all, however sincere we are in our desires, however ready to lament the levity of others, seriously ask our own hearts if we can entirely acquit ourselves of the inconstancy we are so ready to blame. Let us ask if we do not find the charge brought against others all too applicable to ourselves.

Irreverence before or during this sacred solemnity is far more rare than durable improvement after it. Few are so thoughtless as to approach it without a resolve for amendment, but comparatively few carry these resolutions into effect. Fear operates in the previous instance. Why should not love operate in that which follows?

A sporadic spirituality is accompanied with sporadic repentance. This kind of repentance is entered into with much mental reservation. It is partial and disconnected. These fragments of contrition, these broken parcels of penitence, if we intend to resort to the same sins or practices again, is not that sorrow which the Almighty has promised to accept. To render it pleasing to God and efficacious to ourselves, there must be an agreement in the parts, an entireness in the whole web of life. There must be a complete repentance. A quarterly contrition in the four weeks preceding the Holy Communion[1] will not wipe out the daily offence, the hourly negligences of the whole sinful year. Sins half forsaken through fear, and half retained through partially resisted temptation and partially adopted resolution make up but an unprofitable piety.

In the bosom of these professed Christians there is a perpetual conflict between fear and desire. In conversation you will generally find them very fervent in the cause of religion, but it is religion as opposed to infidelity, not as opposed to worldly-mindedness. They defend the worship of God, but they desire to be excused from His *service*. Their heart is the slave of the world, but their blindness hides from them the depravity of that world. They commend piety but dread its requirements. They admit that repentance is necessary, but then how easy it is to find reasons for deferring a necessary evil!

---

[1] Alluding to the practice at that time of observing Holy Communion quarterly.

Who will hastily adopt a painful measure when he can find a creditable pretence for evading it? They censure whatever is ostensibly wrong, but avoiding only part of it, the part they retain robs them of the benefits of their partial renunciation.

We cannot sufficiently admire the wisdom of the Church in enjoining extraordinary acts of devotion and the return of those festivals so happily calculated to produce devotional feelings. Extraordinary repentance of sin is peculiarly suitable to the seasons that record the grand events which sin occasioned, viz. the remembrance of the passion and death of our Lord. But the Church never intended that these stated and strict self-examinations should preclude our habitual self-inspection. It never intended its holy offices to supply the place of general holiness, but to promote it. It intended that these solemn occasions should animate the flame of piety, but it never meant to furnish a reason for neglecting to keep the flame alive till the next Communion service should again kindle the dying embers. It meant that every such season should gladden the heart of the Christian at its approach, but not excuse us from our duty at its departure. It meant to lighten our conscience of the burden of sin, not to encourage us to begin a new score of guilt to be wiped off again at the next festival. It intended to quicken the vigilance of the believer, not to dismiss the guard from his post. If we are not the better for these divinely appointed helps, we are the worse. If we use them as a relief from the diligence which they were intended to promote, we convert our blessings into snares.

This abuse of our advantages arises from not incorporating our devotions into the general habits of our lives. Until our religion becomes an inward motivating force and not simply an external act, we shall not receive the benefit that its forms are meant to give us. It is to those who possess the spirit of Christ that these forms are so valuable. To them the form excites the spirit and the spirit animates the form. Until religion becomes the desire of our hearts, it will not become the business of our lives.

We do not mean that "religion" is to be its actual occupation, but that every portion, every habit, every act of life is to be animated by its spirit, influenced by its principle, governed by its power. The very constitution of our nature and our necessary business with the world naturally fill our hearts and minds with thoughts and ideas over which we have unhappily too little control. We find this to be the case when in our better hours we attempt to give ourselves up to serious reflection. How many intrusions of worldly thoughts, how many impertinent imaginations, not only irrelevant but uncalled for and unwelcome, crowd in upon the mind so forcibly as scarcely to be repelled by our sincerest efforts! How impotent then to repel such images must that mind be which is devoted to worldly pursuits, which yields itself up to them, whose opinions, habits and conduct are willingly put under their influence!

If, as we have observed, faith consists in a new heart and a new spirit, it will become not our occasional act, but our abiding disposition, proving its settled existence in the mind by habitually ordering our thoughts and actions, our devotions and our practice.

Let us not consider a spirit of worldliness as a little infirmity, as a natural and therefore pardonable weakness, a trifling error to be overlooked in consideration of our many good qualities. It is in fact the essence of our other faults: the temperament that stands between us and our salvation. It is the spirit which is in direct opposition to the Spirit of God. Individual sins may more easily be cured, but this is the root of all spiritual disease. A worldly spirit, where it is rooted and cherished, runs through the whole character, insinuates itself in all we say, think and do.

It is this which makes us so dead in devotion, so averse to spiritual things, so forgetful of God, unmindful of eternity, satisfied with ourselves, and so alive to vain and frivolous conversation which excludes intellect almost as much as piety from our general discussions with others.

It is not therefore our more considerable actions alone which require watching, for they seldom occur. They do not form the habit of life in ourselves nor the chief importance of our example to others. It is our *ordinary* behavior, our conduct in common life, our prevailing turn of mind in routine talk by which we shall help or hinder those with whom we associate. It is our conduct in social life which will help to diffuse a spirit of piety or a distaste for it. If we have much influence, this is the place in which particularly to discharge it. If we have little, we have still enough to affect the disposition of our more limited sphere.

If we really believe that it is the design of Christianity to raise us to a participation in the divine nature, the slightest reflection of this elevation of our character would lead us to maintain its dignity in the ordinary relationships of life. We should not so much enquire whether we are transgressing any actual prohibition, as whether we are supporting the dignity of the Christian character, acting suitably to our profession. We might ask whether more exactness in meeting the mundane responsibilities of the day and more correctness in our conversation would produce important results.

The most insignificant people must not undervalue their own influence. Most persons have a little circle of which they are a sort of center. Its smallness may lessen their quantity of good, but does not diminish the duty of using that little influence wisely. Where is the human who is so inconsiderable that he may not in some way benefit others, either by calling their virtues into exercise, or by setting them an example himself? But we are humble in the wrong place. When it is a question of the exhibition of our talents or splendid qualities we are not shy in the display. When a little self-denial is to be exercised, when a little good might be effected by giving a better turn to the conversation, then at once we grow wickedly modest. "Such an insignificant creature as I am can do no good! If I had a higher rank or brighter talents, then indeed my influence might be exerted to some purpose." Under the mask of modesty we justify our passivity and let slip small occasions of promoting the truth. If we all used such occasions, the condition of society might be improved.

The hackneyed question, "What? Must we always be talking about religion?" must have the hackneyed answer: "Far from it!" Talking about religion is not being religious. But we may bring the *spirit* of religion into company and keep it in perpetual operation without making it the subject of conversation. We may be constantly advancing its interests without effort or affectation by giving examples of openness, moderation, humility and forbearance. We may exert our influence by correcting falsehood, checking undue superficiality, discouraging misrepresentation—by approving everything which has a good tendency and, in short, by throwing our whole weight, great or small, on the right side of the scale.

Chapter 5
Prayer

Prayer is the appeal of need to Him who alone can relieve it; the voice of sin to Him who alone can pardon it. It is the urgency of poverty, the prostration of humility, the fervency of penitence, the confidence of trust. It is not eloquence, but earnestness; not the idea of helplessness, but the actual feeling of it; not figures of speech, but compunction of soul. It is the "Lord, save me!" of drowning Peter. (Matt. 14:30) It is the cry of faith to the ear of mercy.

Adoration is the noblest occupation of created beings; confession the natural language of guilty creatures; gratitude the spontaneous expression of pardoned sinners.

Prayer is desire. It is not a conception of the mind, nor a mere effort of the intellect, nor an act of the memory. It is an elevation of the soul towards its Maker, a pressing sense of our own ignorance and infirmity, a consciousness of the perfections of God, of His readiness to hear, of His power to help, of His willingness to save.

It is not an emotion produced in the senses, nor an effect brought about by the imagination, but it is a determination of the will, a pouring out of the heart.

Prayer is the guide to self-knowledge, for it prompts us to look for our sins in order to pray against them. It is a motivation to vigilance, by teaching us to guard against those sins which, through self-examination, we have been enabled to detect.

Prayer is an act both of the understanding and of the heart. The understanding must apply itself to the knowledge of God, or the heart will not be led to the adoration of Him. Prayer would not be a *reasonable* service if the mind was excluded. It must be rational worship, or the human worshippers will not bring to our service the distinguishing feature of our nature, namely our reason. It must be spiritual worship, or it will lack the distinctive quality necessary to make it acceptable to Him who has declared that He will be worshiped "in spirit and in truth."

Prayer in itself is the most powerful means of resisting sin and advancing in holiness. Above all it is right, as everything is which has the authority of Scripture, the command of God and Christ's own example.

There is a perfect consistency in all the ordinances of God; a perfect congruity in the whole scheme of the laws He has decreed. If man were not a corrupt creature, such prayer as the Gospel enjoins would not have been necessary. Had not prayer been an important means for curing those corruptions, a God of perfect wisdom would not have ordered it. He would not have prohibited every thing which tends to inflame and promote those corruptions, if they had not existed, nor would He have commanded everything that is able to diminish and remove them, had not their existence been fatal. Prayer therefore is an indispensable part of His economy and of our obedience.

Some will object to the use of prayer, claiming that it is offending the omniscience of God to suppose that

He must be informed of our need. But no objection could be more hackneyed or futile. We do not pray to *inform* God of our need, but to *express* our sense of need which He already knows. Since He has promised to hear our prayers, it is reasonable that our requests should be made before we can hope that our needs will be met. God does not promise to those who *want* that they shall *have,* but to those who *ask;* nor to those who need that they shall *find,* but to those who *seek.* His previous knowledge of our need is no reason for us to object to prayer. It is, in fact, the true reason for us to pray. He knows our need, for He is Knowledge itself, and He hears our prayers, for He is Goodness itself.

We cannot attain a true understanding of prayer if we remain ignorant of our own nature, of the nature of God as revealed in Scripture, and of our relationship to Him and dependence on Him. If therefore, we do not live in the daily study of the Holy Scriptures, we shall lack the highest motivations for prayer and the best helps for performing it.

One cause, then, of the dullness of many Christians in prayer is their unfamiliarity with the Word of God. They hear it periodically, they read it occasionally, and they are contented to consider it superficially, but they do not endeavor to get their minds infused with its Spirit. They may store their memories with its facts, but they do not impress their hearts with its truths. They do not regard it as the nutriment upon which their spiritual life and growth depend. They do not pray over it. They do not consider all its doctrines as of practical use; they do not cultivate that spiritual discernment which alone can enable us both to claim its promises and to heed its warnings.

In our leisure we too often fritter away our precious moments in trivial, and sometimes, it is to be feared, even in corrupt thoughts. But if we must give the reins to our imagination, let us allow it to range among great and noble objects. Let it stretch forward under the sanction of faith and the anticipation of prophecy, to dwell upon those glorious promises and the tremendous things soon to be realized in the eternal world. These are topics which, under the safe and sober guidance of Scripture, will fix the imagination's largest speculations and sustain its loftiest flights. The same Scripture, while it expands and elevates the mind, will keep it subject to the dominion of truth. It will teach it that its boldest excursions must fall infinitely short of the astonishing realities of a future state.

Although we cannot pray with too deep a sense of sin, we may make our sins too exclusively the object of our prayers. While, with a self-abasing eye, we keep our own corruptions in view, let us look with equal intensity on that mercy which cleanses from all sin. Let our prayers be with humility, but let them not be full of complaints. When we dwell upon no other thought than that we are but rebels, the hopelessness of pardon hardens us into disloyalty. Let us look to the mercy of the King as well as to the rebellion of the subject. If we contemplate His grace as displayed in the Gospel, then our humility will increase, and our despair will vanish. Gratitude will create affection. "We love Him because He first loved us." (I John 4:19)

Let us then always keep our unworthiness in view as a reason why we stand in need of the mercy of God in Christ; but never plead it as a reason why we should not draw near to Him to implore that mercy.

In prayer then, the perfections of God, and especially His mercies as revealed in our redemption, should occupy our thoughts as much as our sins; our obligations to Him as much as our departures from Him. We should keep in our hearts a constant sense of our own weakness, not for the purpose of discouraging the mind and depressing the spirit, but to drive us out of ourselves to search for divine aid and relief. We should contemplate our infirmity in order to inspire us to look for His strength and to seek that power from God which we vainly look for in ourselves. We do not tell a sick friend of his danger in order to grieve or frighten him, but to induce him to seek the help of his physician.

Among the arguments which have been brought against serious piety is that it teaches us to despair. In one sense this is true, but not in the sense in which the argument is intended. True piety teaches us to despair indeed of ourselves, while it inspires faith in our Redeemer, which is the true antidote to despair. Faith quickens the doubting spirit while it humbles the presumptuous one. The lowly Christian takes comfort in the blessed promise that God will never forsake them that are His. The presumptuous man is equally right in the doctrine, but wrong in applying it. He takes that comfort to himself which was meant for another class of characters. The wrong use of Scriptural promises is the cause of much error and delusion.

Some devout enthusiasts have fallen into error by asserting that God is to be loved exclusively for Himself with an absolute renunciation of any advantage to ourselves. Yet that prayer cannot be considered selfish which involves God's glory with our own happiness, and makes His will the law of our requests. Though we are to desire the glory of God supremely, He has graciously permitted, commanded, and invited us to attach our own happiness to this primary purpose. The Bible exhibits a beautiful combination of both. This protects us from the danger of unnaturally renouncing our own benefit for the promotion of God's glory on the one hand, and on the other, from seeking any happiness independent of Him, and underived from Him. In enjoining us to love Him supremely, He has connected an unspeakable blessing with a paramount duty, the highest privilege with the most positive command.

What a triumph for the humble Christian to be assured that "the high and lofty One who inhabits eternity," (Isa. 57:15) condescends at the same time to dwell in the heart of the contrite! To know that God is the God of our life, to *know* that we are even invited to take the Lord for our God—to receive His promises, to accept His invitations, to know God as our portion—must surely be more pleasing to our heavenly Father than for us to separate our happiness from His glory. To disconnect our interests from His goodness is at once to diminish His perfections and to obscure the brightness of our own hopes. The declarations of inspired writers are confirmed by the authority of the heavenly hosts. They proclaim that the glory of God and the happiness of His creatures do not interfere with each other, but rather are connected with each other. We know of one anthem composed and sung by angels, and this most harmoniously combines "glory to God in the highest" with "peace on earth and good will to men." (Luke 2:14)

"The beauty of Scripture," says one of the great Reformers, "consists in pronouns." This God is *our* God— God, even our *own* God shall bless us. How delightful to glorify Him who is perfect excellence, and to love Him for directing this excellence to our own happiness! Here modesty would be ingratitude, and indifference would be rebellion. It would be severing ourselves from Him in whom we live and move and have our being. It would be dissolving the connection which He has condescended to establish between Himself and His creatures.

It has been justly observed that the Scriptural saints make this union the chief ground of their grateful exultation—"*My* strength," "*my* fortress," "*my* deliverer!" "Let the God of *my* salvation be exalted!" (Ps. 18:1,2,46) Take away the pronoun and substitute the article *the,* and see how comparatively cold is the impression! The fullness of joy arises from the intimacy and the endearment of the relationship.

Yet the joy is not diminished when the individual Christian blesses his God as "the God of all them that trust in Him." (cf. Ps. 31:14) All general blessings, he will say, all providential mercies, are ours individually. They are ours as completely as if no other shared in their enjoyment—life, light, the earth and heavens, the sun and stars, whatever sustains the body, and recreates the spirit! Our obligation is as great as if the mercy had been made purely for us. As great?—no, it is greater, because it is augmented by an awareness of the millions of other souls who also participate in the blessing. The Lord is *my* Savior as completely as if He had redeemed only me. That He has redeemed a "great multitude which no man can number, of all nations and kindreds and people and tongues" (Rev. 7:9) is a general participation without any individual diminishment. Each has all.

In adoring the Providence of God, we are apt to be struck with what is new and unusual, while we too much overlook those long, habitual and uninterrupted mercies of God. But common mercies, if less striking are more valuable, because we have them always and because others share in them as well. The ordinary blessings of life are overlooked for the very reason that they ought to be most prized, because they are most uniformly bestowed. They are most essential to our support, and when once they are withdrawn we begin to find that they are also most essential to our well-being. Nothing increases the worth of a blessing like its removal, whereas its continuance should have taught us its value. We demand novelties to awaken our gratitude, not considering that it is the duration of mercies which enhances their value. We want fresh excitements. We consider mercies long enjoyed as things to be taken for granted, as things to which we have a presumptive claim, as if God had no right to withdraw what He had once given.

The sun shone unceasingly from the day that God created it, but this is no less a stupendous exertion of power than the incident when the hand which fixed it in the heavens, once commanded through His servant, "Sun, stand thou still upon Gibeon." (Josh. 10:12) That the sun has gone on in its strength, enduring in its uninterrupted mission, and "rejoicing as a giant to run his course," is a more astonishing exhibition of omnipotence than that it should have been once suspended by the hand which set it in motion. That the established laws of nature should have been for one day interrupted to serve a particular occasion, is smaller wonder and certainly a less substantial blessing, than that in such a multitude of ages they should have pursued their appointed course, for the comfort of the whole creation:

> *For ever singing as they shine*
> *The hand that made us is divine.*

As the affections of the Christian ought to be set on things above, so it is for those things that his prayers will be chiefly addressed. God, in promising to "give those who delight in Him the desire of their heart," (Ps. 37:4) could never mean temporal things, for these may be desired improperly. The promise relates principally to spiritual blessings. He not only gives us these mercies, but the very desire to obtain them is also His gift. Here our prayer requires no qualifying, no conditioning, no limitation. We cannot err in our choice, for God Himself is the object of it. We cannot pray too eagerly unless it is possible to love Him too well, or to please Him too much.

Though lawful in themselves, we should pray for worldly

comforts, and for blessing on our earthly plans conditionally and with reservation. After having been earnest in our requests for them, it may happen that when we come to the petition, "Thy will be done" we may in these very words be praying that our previous petitions may not be granted. This brief request contains the vital principle, the essential spirit of prayer. God shows His generosity by encouraging us to ask most earnestly for the greatest things, by promising that the smaller "shall be added unto us." (Matt. 6:33) We therefore acknowledge His liberality most when we request the highest favors. He manifests His infinite superiority to earthly fathers chiefly by delighting to confer spiritual gifts—gifts which *they* desire for their children less eagerly than those worldly benefits on which God sets so little value.

Nothing short of a sincere devotion to God can enable us to maintain a stability of mind under unstable circumstances. We murmur when we do not receive the things for which we ask amiss, not knowing that they are withheld by the same mercy which grants the things that are good for us. Things good in themselves may not be good for us. A resigned spirit is the proper disposition to prepare us for receiving mercies, or for having them denied. Resignation of soul is always in readiness even when not in action, whereas an impatient mind is a spirit of animosity, always prepared to revolt when the will of the sovereign is in opposition to that of the subject. This seditious principle is the unfailing characteristic of an unrenewed mind.

A sincere love of God will make us thankful when our supplications are granted, and patient and cheerful when they are denied. He who feels his heart rise against any divine dispensation ought not to rest until by serious meditation and earnest prayer it be molded into submission. Then he will recollect the many instances in which, if his importunity had prevailed, the thing which ignorance requested, and wisdom denied, would have insured his misery. Every fresh disappointment will teach him to distrust himself and confide in God. Experience will instruct him that there may be a better way of hearing our requests than that of granting them. Happy for us that He to whom they are addressed knows which is best, and acts upon that knowledge.

> *Still lift for good the supplicating voice,*
> *But leave to Heaven the measure and the choice;*
> *Implore His aid, in His decisions rest,*
> *Secure whate'er He gives, He gives the best.*

We should endeavor to make of our private devotions effectual remedies for our own particular sins. Prayer against sin in general is too indefinite. We must bring it home to our own heart, else we may be confessing another man's sins and overlooking our own. If we have any predominant fault, we should pray more especially against that fault. If we pray for any virtue of which we particularly stand in need, we should dwell on our own deficiencies in that virtue, until our souls become deeply desirous of it. As the recounting of our wants tends to keep up a sense of our dependence, the recollection of the mercies we have received will tend to keep alive a sense of gratitude. Indiscriminate petitions, confessions, and thanksgivings leave the mind to wander in indefinite devotion and generalities.

Of the blessings which attend urgency in prayer the Gospel is abundantly explicit. God perhaps delays in granting our request in order that we may persevere in asking. He may require importunity for our own sakes, that the frequency and urgency of the petition may bring our hearts into that attitude to which He will be most favorable.

As we ought to live in a spirit of obedience to His

commands, so we should live in an attitude of waiting for His blessing on our prayers, and in a spirit of gratitude when we have obtained it. This is that "preparation of the heart" which would always keep us in a posture for duty. If we desert the duty because an immediate blessing does not visibly attend it, it shows that we do not serve God out of conscience but selfishness—that we begrudge expending on Him that service which brings us no immediate reward. Even if He does not grant our petition, let us never be tempted to withdraw our prayer.

Our reluctant devotions may remind us of the remark of a certain great political wit who apologized for arriving late at Parliament. He had been detained, he said, while watching a party of soldiers *drag a volunteer* to his duty. How many excuses do we find for not being on time! How many apologies for brevity! How many evasions for neglect! How unwilling, too often, are we to come into the divine Presence, how reluctant to remain in it! Those hours which are least valuable for business, which are least seasonable for pleasure, we commonly give to prayer. Our energies which were so exerted when we were among our friends or business associates, tend to sink when we approach the divine Presence. Our hearts, which were all animated in some frivolous conversation, become cold and lethargic, as if it were the natural property of devotion to freeze the affections. The sluggish body sympathizes with the unwilling mind, and each promotes the deadness of the other. Both are slow in listening to the call of duty. Both are soon weary in performing it. As prayer requires all our energies, so we too often feel as if there were a conspiracy of body, soul and spirit to discourage and disable us for it.

When the heart is once sincerely turned to God, we need not, every time we pray, examine every truth and seek for conviction over and over again. We may assume that those doctrines are still true which have already been proven to us. As we keep these doctrines firmly fixed in our minds, we will discover a love so intimate that the convictions of the understanding will become the affections of the heart.

To be deeply impressed with a few fundamental truths, to digest them thoroughly, to meditate on them seriously, to pray over them fervently, to get them deeply rooted in the heart, will be more productive to faith and holiness than to labor after variety or cleverness. The indulgence of imagination will distract rather than edify. Searching after ingenious thoughts will divert the attention from God to ourselves, rather than promote fixedness of thought, singleness of intention, and devotedness of spirit. Whatever is subtle and refined is in danger of being unscriptural. If we do not guard the mind it will learn to wander in quest of novelties. It will learn to set more value on original thoughts than devout affections. It is the business of prayer to cast down imaginations which gratify the natural activity of the mind, while they leave the heart unhumbled.

We should confine ourselves to the present business of the present moment. We should keep the mind in a state of perpetual dependence. "Now is the accepted time." "Today we must hear His voice." "Give us *this* day our daily bread." (cf. II Cor. 6:2; Heb. 3:7; Matt. 6:11) The manna will not keep until tomorrow. Tomorrow will have its own needs and must have its own petitions. Tomorrow we must seek the bread of heaven afresh.

We should, however, avoid coming to our devotions with unprepared minds. We should always be laying up materials for prayer by a diligent course of serious reading, by treasuring up in our minds the most important truths. If we rush into the divine Presence with a vacant or unprepared mind, with a heart full of the world, we shall feel no disposition or qualification for the work we are about to engage in. We cannot expect that our petitions will be heard or granted. There must be some congruity between the heart and the object, some affinity between the state of our minds and the business in which they are employed, if we would expect success in the work.

We are often deceived as to the underlying motive and the effect of our prayers. When from some external cause the heart is glad, the spirits light, the thoughts ready, the tongue effusive, a spontaneous eloquence is the result. We are pleased with this and we are willing to consider this ready flow as piety.

On the other hand, when the mind is dejected, the spirits low, the thoughts confused, when appropriate words do not readily present themselves, we are apt to accuse our hearts of lack of fervor. We lament our weakness and mourn that because we have had no pleasure in praying our prayers have not ascended to the throne of mercy. In both cases we may judge ourselves unfairly. These ill-expressed petitions may find more acceptance than the florid talk with which we were so well satisfied. The latter consisted, it may be, of shining thoughts, floating on the fancy, eloquent words dwelling only on the lips. The former was the sighing of a contrite heart, abased by the feeling of its own unworthiness, and awed by the perfections of a holy and heart-searching God. The heart is dissatisfied with its own dull and tasteless repetitions, which, even with all their imperfections, Infinite Goodness may perhaps hear with favor. We may not only be elated with the fluency, but even with the fervency of our prayers. Vanity may grow out of the very act of renouncing it, and we may begin to feel proud at having humbled ourselves so eloquently.

There is however, a strain and spirit of prayer equally distinct from that facility and profuseness or dryness about which we have been speaking. There is a simple, solid, devout strain of prayer in which the supplicant is so filled and occupied with a sense of his own dependence, and of the importance of the things for which we ask, in which we are so persuaded of the power and grace of God through Christ to give us those things, that while we are engaged in it, we do not merely imagine, but feel assured that God is near us as a reconciled Father. Thus every burden and doubt are taken off our minds. "He knows," as St John expresses it, "that he has the petitions he desired of God," and feels the truth of that promise "while they are yet speaking I will hear." (I John 5:15; Isa. 65:24) This is the perfection of prayer.

Chapter 6
Cultivating a Devotional Spirit

To maintain a devotional spirit, two things are especially necessary: to cultivate the disposition to it and to avoid whatever is unfavorable to it. Frequent retirement and recollection are indispensable, together with such a general course of reading as will help to maintain it. We should avoid as much as possible the kind of company amusements which will excite feeling which it is our duty to subdue—all those feelings which it is our constant duty to suppress.

Here we may venture to observe that if some things which are apparently innocent and do not assume an alarming aspect or bear a dangerous character—things which most careful people affirm to be safe for them— if we find that these things stir up in us improper thoughts and feelings, if they lessen our love for devotion or infringe upon our time for performing them, if they wind our heart a little more around the world, then let no belief in their alleged innocence tempt us to indulge in them. It matters little to *our* security what they are to others. Our business is with ourselves. Our responsibility is on our own heads. Others cannot know the side on which we are most vulnerable. Let our own unbiased judgment and our own experience decide for our own conduct.

Speaking of books, we cannot help noticing a very prevalent sort of reading which is just as productive of evil and just as unhelpful to moral and mental improvement as that which carries a more blatant face of wickedness. We cannot confine our censure to the more corrupt writings which deprave the heart and poison the principles. Their depravity is so obvious that no warning here, it is presumed, *can* be necessary. But if justice forbids us to confuse the insipid with the mischievous, the idle with the vicious, still we can only admit of shades of difference, deep shades though they may be. These works, though comparatively harmless, still lower the taste, slacken the intellectual nerve, set imagination loose and send it gadding among low and unworthy objects. They not only waste the time which should be given to better things, but gradually destroy all taste for better things. They drag the mind to their own standard, and give it a sluggish reluctance, perhaps even a moral incapacity, for anything above their level. The mind, by its long habit of stooping to these levels, loses its uprightness. It becomes so low and narrow by the littleness of the things which engage it that it requires a painful effort to lift itself high enough, or to open itself wide enough to embrace great and noble objects. The appetite is weakened or polluted. The faculties which might have been expanding in works of science or soaring with the contemplation of genius, become satisfied with the irrelevancies of the most ordinary fiction. They lose their relish for the severity of truth, the elegance of taste and the soberness of religion. Lulled in the torpor of repose, the intellect dozes and enjoys its waking dream.

In avoiding books which excite the passions, it may

seem strange to include even some devotional works. Yet those which merely kindle warm feelings are not always the safest. Let us rather prefer those which, while they tend to raise a devotional spirit, awaken the affections without disordering them. Let us prefer those that purify the desires while elevating them, that show us our own nature and lay open its corruptions. Let us read those that show us the malignity of sin, the deceitfulness of our hearts, the feebleness of our best resolutions—those that teach us to pull off the mask from the fairest appearances and uncover every hiding place where some lurking evil would conceal itself. Let us choose those that show us not what we appear to others but what we really are, that cooperate with our interior feeling and point out our absolute need of a Redeemer, lead us to seek Him for pardon from a conviction that we have no other refuge, no other salvation. Let us be conversant with such writings as teach us that while we desire the remission of our sins, we must not desire the remission of our duties. Let us seek for a Savior who will not only deliver us from the punishment of sin, but from its dominion also.

Let us always bear in mind that the *end of prayer is not answered* when the prayer is finished. We should regard prayer as a means to a further end. The act of prayer is not sufficient. We must cultivate a *spirit* of prayer. And though when the actual devotion is over we cannot always be thinking of heavenly things in the midst of company and business, yet we must endeavor to maintain the desire to return to them.

The proper disposition toward prayer should precede the act. It should be wrought in the mind before the exercise is begun. To bring a proud temper to a humble prayer, a luxurious habit to a self-denying prayer, or a worldly disposition to a spiritually-minded prayer is a positive anomaly. A habit is more powerful than an act, and a previously indulged temper during the day will not be fully counteracted by the exercise of a few minutes' devotion at night.

That the habitual tendency of one's life should be the preparation for the spoken prayer is naturally suggested to us by our blessed Redeemer in His Sermon on the Mount. He announced the precepts of holiness and their corresponding beatitudes. He gave the spiritual exposition of the Law, the directions for alms-giving, the exhortation to love our enemies. He gave the essence and spirit of the whole Ten Commandments before He delivered His own divine prayer. Let us learn from this that the preparation of prayer is therefore to live in all those pursuits which we may safely beg of God to bless, and in a resistance against all those temptations into which we pray not to be led.

If God is to be the center to which our hearts are tending, every line in our lives must meet in Him. With this point in view there will be a harmony between our prayers and our practice, a consistency between devotion and conduct. For the beauty of the Christian life consists not in parts (however good in themselves) which tend to separate views and lead to different ends. It arises rather from its being one intact, uniform and connected plan, "joined and knit together by every joint with which it is supplied," (Eph. 4:16) and of which all the parts terminate in this one grand ultimate point—God Himself.

The design of prayer therefore as we have observed, is not merely to make us devout while we are engaged in it, but that its fragrance may be diffused through all the rest of the day and enter into all its occupations and tempers. Its results must not be partial or limited to easy and pleasant duties, but must extend to those that are less appealing. For instance, when we pray for our enemies, the prayer must be rendered practical and made a means of softening our spirit and cooling our resentment toward them. If we deserve their enmity, the true spirit of prayer will cause us to endeavor to cure the fault which has provoked it. If we do not deserve it, it will cause us to strive for a reconciling spirit in us, so as to avoid occasion for further offense. There is no such softener of animosity, no such allayer of hatred as sincere, heart-felt prayer.

It is obvious that the precept to pray without ceasing can never mean to require a continual course of actual prayer. But while it enjoins us to embrace all proper occasions for performing this sacred duty (or rather for claiming this valuable privilege), it plainly implies that we should try to keep constantly within ourselves that sense of the divine presence which shall maintain a prayerful frame of mind. In order to do this we should accustom our minds to reflection. We should encourage serious thoughts. A good thought barely passing through the mind will make little impression on it. We must seize it, constrain it to remain with us, expand, amplify and, as it were, take it to pieces. It must be distinctly unfolded and carefully examined, or it will leave no precise idea. It must be fixed and incorporated, or it will produce no practical effect. We must not dismiss it until it has left some trace on the mind, until it has made some impression on the heart.

On the other hand, if we give way to a loose, ungoverned fancy at other times and abandon our minds to frivolous thoughts, if we fill them with corrupt images and cherish sensual ideas during the rest of the day, can we expect that none of these images will intrude, that the "temple into which these foul things" have been invited will be cleansed at a moment's notice? Can we hope that our worldly thoughts will recede and give place at once to pure and holy ones? Will that Spirit, grieved by impurity or defied by unclean humor, return with His warm beams and cheering influences to the contaminated mansion from which He has been driven out?

We cannot, by retiring to our prayer closet, change our natures as we do our clothes. The disposition we carry there will be likely to remain with us. We have no right to expect that a new temper will meet us at the door. We can only hope that the spirit we bring to it will be cherished and improved. It is not easy, rather it is not *possible,* to graft genuine devotion on a life of an opposite tendency. We cannot delight ourselves regularly for a few stated moments in the God whom we have not been serving through the day. We may indeed quiet our conscience and take up the employment of prayer. But we cannot take up the state of mind which will make such employment beneficial to ourselves or the prayer acceptable to God if all the previous day we have been careless of ourselves and unmindful of our Maker. They will not pray differently from the rest of the world who do not live differently.

What a contradiction it is to lament the weakness, misery and corruption of our nature in our devotion and then to rush into a life—though not perhaps of vice, yet of indulgences that can only increase that weakness, misery and corruption! There is either no meaning in our prayers or no sense in our conduct. In the one we mock God; in the other we deceive ourselves.

Will not he who keeps up a habitual conversation with his Maker, who is vigilant in thought, self-denying in action, who strives to keep his heart from wrong desires and his mind from vain imaginations, bring a more prepared spirit, a more collected mind to the occasion of prayer? Will he not feel more delight in this devout exercise and reap more benefit from it than the one who lives at random, prays from custom, and who cannot truly say, "O God, my heart is steadfast"? (Ps. 57:7)

We speak here not to the self-sufficient formalist or the careless pleasure-seeker. Among those to whom we now speak are to be found those who are amiable and virtuous. Their characters are so engaging, so evidently made for better things, capable of reaching high degrees of excellence, so formed to give the tone to Christian practice as well as to ideas, that we cannot resist taking a tender interest in their welfare. It is our prayer that they may yet reach the elevation for which they were intended and hold up a uniform and consistent pattern of "whatsoever things are pure, honest, just, lovely, and of good report"! (Phil. 4:8) That can be done, as St Paul reminds us, only by *thinking* on these things. Things can only influence our practice as they engage our attention.

Miscalculating the relative value of things is one of the greatest errors of our moral life. We estimate them in an inverse proportion to their value as well as to their duration. We lavish earnest and durable thoughts on things so trifling that they deserve little regard, so brief that they perish with the using, while we bestow only slight attention on things of infinite worth, only transient thoughts on things of eternal duration.

Those who are conscientious enough to keep a regular pattern of devotion, and who yet allow themselves at the same time to go on in a course of worldly amusements which encourage exactly the opposite spirit, are inconceivably multiplying their own difficulties. They are eagerly heaping up fuel in the day on a fire which they intend to extinguish in the evening. They are voluntarily adding to the temptations against which they intend to pray for grace to resist. To acknowledge at the same time that we find it hard to serve God as we ought, and yet to be systematically indulging habits which must naturally increase the difficulty, makes our characters almost ridiculous, while it renders our duty almost unmanageable.

While some make their way more difficult by those very indulgences with which they think to cheer and refresh it, the determined Christian becomes his own pioneer. He makes his path easy by voluntarily clearing it of the obstacles which hold back his progress.

These habitual indulgences seem a contradiction to the law that one virtue always involves another, for we cannot labor after any grace (that of prayer, for instance) without resisting whatever is opposite to it. If we lament that it is hard to serve God, let us not continue to heap up mountains in our way by indulging in such pursuits and habits that make a small labor an insurmountable one.

We may often judge ourselves by the result than by the act of prayer. Our very defects, our coldness, deadness, and wanderings may leave more contrition on the soul than the happiest turn of thought. The feeling of our needs, the confession of our sins, the acknowledgment of our dependence, the renunciation of ourselves, our supplication for mercy, the heartfelt entreaty for the aid of the Spirit, the relinquishment of our own will, our resolutions of better obedience—these are the subjects in which the supplicant should be engaged. Can they absorb our thoughts if many of the intervening hours are passed in pursuits of a totally different complexion? Will the cherished vanities go at our bidding? Will the needed frame of mind return at our calling? Do we find our emotions so obedient, our passions so subservient in the other concerns of life? If not, what reason do we have to expect their compliance when we come to pray? We should therefore endeavor to believe as we pray, to think as we pray, to feel as we pray, and to act as we pray. Prayer must not be a solitary, independent exercise, but one interwoven with many others. Prayer must be inseparably connected with that golden chain of Christian duties as one of its most important links.

Service must have its period as well as devotion. We were sent into this world to act as well as to pray. Active duties must be performed as well as devout exercises. Even relaxation must have its place; only let us be careful that the indulgence of the one does not destroy the effect of the other, that our pleasures do not encroach on the time or deaden the spirit of our devotions. Let us be careful that our cares, occupations and amusements may be always such that we are not afraid to implore God's blessing on them. This is the criterion of their *safety* and of our duty. Let us endeavor to maintain in every occupation a growing feeling of loving, serving and pleasing God.

One other reason why we should live in the perpetual use of prayer seems to be that our blessed Redeemer, having given both the example and command "to pray and not to faint," (Luke 18:1) while He was on earth, still condescends to be our Intercessor in heaven. Can we ever cease petitioning for ourselves when we believe that He never ceases interceding for us? (Heb. 7:25)

If, sadly, we find little pleasure in this holy exercise, that is no reason for discontinuing it. Indeed, it affords the strongest argument for persevering! That which was at first a form will become a pleasure. That which was a burden will become a privilege. That which we impose upon ourselves as a medicine will become necessary nourishment. That which is now short and superficial will become bountiful and solid. The chariot wheel is warmed by its own motion. Use will make easy what was at first painful. Instead of repining over the act of prayer, we shall be unhappy at its omission. When we have been sick and weak from lack of exercise, we persevere through that weakness to regain our strength. The effort which was put forth because it was necessary for health is continued because the feeling of renewed strength makes it delightful.

Chapter 7
Do We Really Love God?

Our love to God arises out of our emptiness; God's love to us out of His fullness. Our impoverishment draws us to that power which can relieve and to that goodness which can bless us. His overflowing love delights to make us partakers of the bounties He graciously imparts. We can only be said to love God when we endeavor to glorify Him, when we desire a participation of His nature, when we study to imitate His perfections.

We are sometimes inclined to suspect the love of God to us, while we too little suspect our own lack of love to Him. Yet if we examine the evidence, as we should examine any common question, what real instances can we produce of our love to Him? And what imaginable instance can we not produce of His love to us? If neglect, forgetfulness, ingratitude, disobedience, coldness in our affections and deadness in our duty are evidences of our lack of love to Him, such evidences we can abundantly show. If life and the catalogue of countless mercies that make life pleasant be proofs of His love to us, these He has given us in abundance. If life eternal, if blessedness that knows no measure and no end, be proofs of love, these He has given us in promise.

It must be an irksome thing to serve a Master whom we do not love, a Master whom we are compelled to obey, though we think His requisitions hard, and His commands unreasonable. Now every Christian must obey God, whether he loves Him or not. He must act always in His sight, whether he delights in Him or not. But to a heart of any feeling, to a spirit of any liberality, nothing is so grating as constrained obedience. To love God, to serve Him because we love Him, is therefore no less our highest happiness than our most bounden duty. Love makes all labor light. We serve with enthusiasm where we love with sincerity.

When the heart is devoted to God, we do not need to be perpetually reminded of our obligations to obey Him. They present themselves spontaneously and we fulfill them readily. We think not so much of the service as of the One served. The motivation which suggests the work inspires the pleasure. To neglect it would be an injury to our own sense of integrity. The performance is the gratification, and the omission is both a pain to the conscience and a wound to the affections.

Though we cannot be always thinking of God, we may be always employed in His service. There must be intervals of our communion with Him, but there must be no intermission of our attachment to Him. The tender father who labors for his children does not always think his thoughts about them. He cannot always be talking with them, yet he is always engaged in promoting their interests. His affection for them is an inwoven principle, proven by the diligence with which he serves them.

"Thou shalt love the Lord thy God with all thy heart," (Deut. 6:5) is the primary law of our faith. Yet how apt are we to complain that we *cannot* love God, that we cannot maintain a devout relationship with Him! But would God,

who is all justice, have commanded that of which He knew
we were incapable? Would He who is all mercy have made
our eternal happiness to depend on something which He
knew was out of our power to perform? Would He have
given the exhortation, and withheld the capacity? This
would be to charge omniscience with folly, and infinite
goodness with injustice. No, when He made duty and
happiness inseparable, He neither made our duty
unmanageable, nor our happiness unattainable. But we
are continually flying to false refuges, clinging to false
holds, resting on false supports. They are certain to
disappoint us, and are weak and fail us, but they are
numerous, so that when one fails, another presents itself.
Eventually they slip from under us. We never suspect how
much we rested upon them. Life glides away in a perpetual
succession of these false dependencies.

There is, as we have elsewhere observed, a striking
analogy between the natural and spiritual life. The
weakness and helplessness of the Christian resembles that
of the infant. Neither of them becomes strong, vigorous
and full grown at once, but rather, through a long and
often painful course. This keeps up a sense of dependence,
and accustoms us to lean on the hand which fosters us.
There is in both cases an imperceptible chain of
interrelated events, by which we are carried on insensibly
to maturity. The operation, though not always obvious,
is always progressive. By attempting to walk alone we
discover our weakness, and the experience of that
weakness humbles us. Every fall drives us back to the
sustaining hand, whose assistance we vainly flattered
ourselves we no longer needed.

In some tranquil moments we are tempted to think
that faith has made an entire conquest over our heart,
that we have renounced the dominion of the world, have
conquered our attachment to earthly things. We flatter
ourselves that nothing can now again obstruct our entire

submission. But we know not of what spirit we are. We say this in the calm of repose, and in the stillness of the passions, when our path is smooth, our prospect smiling, when danger is distant, temptation absent and when we have many comforts and no trials. Suddenly, some loss, some disappointment, some privation tears off the mask and reveals us to ourselves. We at once discover that though the smaller fibers and lesser roots which fasten us down to earth may have been loosened by preceding storms, yet our substantial hold on earth is not shaken, the tap root is not cut. We are still rooted to the soil, and still stronger tempests must be sent to make us let go our hold.

It might be useful to state our own case as strongly to ourselves as if it were the case of another. How indignant, for instance, should we feel (though we ourselves make the complaint) to be told by others that we do not love our Maker and Preserver. But let us put the question fairly to ourselves. Do we really love Him? Do we love Him with a supreme affection? Is there no friend, no child, no reputation, no pleasure, no society, no possession which we do not prefer to Him? It is easy to affirm in a general way that there is not. But let us particularize the question— bring it home to our own hearts in some actual instance, in some tangible shape. Let us commune with our own consciences, with our own feelings, with our own experience. Let us question pointedly, and answer honestly. Let us not be more ashamed to detect the fault than to have been guilty of it.

This then will commonly be the result. Let the friend, child, reputation, possession or pleasure be endangered, but especially let it be taken away by some stroke of Providence. Immediately the scales fall from our eyes. We see, we feel, we acknowledge with brokenness of heart that though we did love God, we did not love Him above all else, and that we loved the blessing still more. But this is one of the cases in which the goodness of God brings us to repentance. By the operation of His grace the return of the gift brings back the heart to the Giver. The Almighty by His Spirit takes possession of the temple from which the idol is driven out. God is reinstated in His rightful place and becomes the supreme and undisputed Lord of our lives.

There are two requirements for our proper enjoyment of every earthly blessing which God bestows on us—a thankful reflection on the goodness of the Giver and a deep sense of the unworthiness of the receiver. The first would make us grateful, the second humble.

How many seem to show their lack of trust in God, that "He is not in all their thoughts," by leaving Him entirely out of their concerns! They arrange their affairs without any reference to Him, relying on their own unassisted wisdom, contriving and acting independently of God. They expect prosperity in the end, without seeking His direction at the outset, and taking to themselves the whole honor of the success without any recognition of His hand. Do they not thus virtually imitate what Sophocles has his blustering Atheist boast? "Let other men," he said, "expect to conquer with the assistance of the gods, I intend to gain honor without them." The Christian will instead rejoice to ascribe the glory of his prosperity to the hand of God.

Incidents and occasions arise every day which call on us to trust in God, and furnish us with occasions to testify to the character and conduct of the Almighty in the government of human affairs. Yet there is no duty which we perform with less zeal. Strange, that we should treat the Lord of heaven and earth with less confidence than we exercise towards each other! It is astounding that we should vindicate the honor of a common acquaintance with more fervor than that of our insulted Maker and Preserver!

If we hear a friend accused of any act of injustice—though we cannot bring any positive proof why he should be acquitted of this specific charge—we resent the injury inflicted upon his character. We clear him of the individual allegation on the ground of his general conduct. We can recount the numerous instances of his integrity on other occasions, and thereby we conclude that he cannot be guilty of the alleged injustice. But when we presume to judge the Most High, instead of defending Him on the same grounds, instead of thinking, as in the case of our friend, of the thousand instances we have formerly tasted of His kindness, instead of giving God the same credit we give to His erring creature, and inferring from His past goodness that what He is doing in the present circumstances must be consistent, we cannot explain how. We mutinously accuse Him of inconsistency and of injustice. We admit virtually the most monstrous contradiction in the character of the perfect God.

But revelation has furnished a clue to the intricate labyrinth which seems to involve the acts of God which we impiously question. It unrolls the volume of divine providence, lays open the mysterious map of infinite wisdom and throws a bright light on the darkest dealings of God. The truth of God points to that blessed region, where to all who have truly loved and served Him every apparent wrong shall be proved to have been unimpeachably right, every affliction a mercy, and the severest trials the choicest blessings.

Sin has made us so blind that the glory of God is concealed from us by the very means which would display it. That train of second causes—His very works and dealings with us—which He has so marvelously disposed, obstructs our view of Himself. We are so filled with wonder at the immediate effect, that our short sight does not perceive Him as the first cause. To see Him as He is, is reserved to be the happiness of a better world. We shall then indeed "admire Him in His saints, and in all them that believe." (2 Thess. 1:10) We shall see how necessary it was for those whose bliss is now so perfect, to have been poor, and despised, and oppressed. We shall see why the "ungodly were in such prosperity." (Ps. 73:3) Let us give God credit here for what we shall then fully know. Let us adore now for what we shall understand hereafter.

They who take up faith on a false ground will never adhere to it. If they adopt it merely for the peace and pleasantness it brings, they will desert it as soon as they find their adherence to it will bring them into difficulty, distress, or discredit. It will never do therefore, to attempt making proselytes by hanging out false colors. The Christian "endures as seeing Him who is invisible." (Heb. 11:27) He who adopts faith for the sake of immediate enjoyment, will not do a virtuous action that is disagreeable to himself, nor resist a temptation that is alluring. There is no sure basis for virtue but the love of God in Christ Jesus, and the bright hope for which that love is pledged. Without this, as soon as the paths of piety become rough and thorny, we shall begin looking for pleasanter pastures.

Faith however, has her own peculiar advantages. In the transaction of all worldly affairs there are many and great difficulties. There may be several ways from which to choose. Those who have no faith are not always certain which of these ways is the best. Persons with the deepest comprehension are full of doubt and perplexity. Their minds are undecided how to act, lest while they pursue one road, they may be neglecting another which might better have conducted them to their desired destination.

For the Christian the case is different, and in this respect, easy. As a Christian can have but one object in view, he is also certain there is but one way of attaining it. Where there is but one end, it prevents all possibility of choosing wrong. Where there is but one road, it takes away all perplexity as to which course to pursue. We may often wander wide of the mark, but this is not from any lack of plainness in the path, but from the perverseness of our will in not choosing it, and from the indolence of our minds in not following it up.

In our attachments to even the most innocent earthly things there is always a danger of excess. But with regard to the love of God we are perfectly exempt from this danger, for there is no possibility of excess in our love to that Being who has demanded the *whole heart.* Had God required only a portion, even were it a large portion, we might be perplexed about deciding the amount. We might be plotting how large a part we might dare to keep back without absolutely forfeiting our safety. We might be haggling for deductions, bargaining for discounts, and be perpetually compromising with our Maker. But the injunction is entire, the command is definite and the portion is unequivocal. It is so distinct a claim, so imperative a requirement of *all* the faculties of the mind and strength, *all* the affections of the heart and soul, that there is not the least opening left for dispute—no place for anything but absolute, unreserved compliance.

Everything which relates to God is infinite. We must therefore, while we keep our hearts humble, keep our aims high. Our highest services are indeed but finite, imperfect. But as God is unlimited in goodness, He should have our unlimited love. The best we can offer is poor, but let us not withhold that best. He deserves incomparably more than we have to give. Let us not give Him less than all. If He has ennobled our corrupt nature with spiritual desires, let us not refuse their noblest aspirations. Let Him not behold us so prodigally lavishing our affections on the smallest of His bounties that we have nothing left for Himself. As God's standard of everything is high, let us endeavor to live for Him with the highest intention of mind. Let us obey Him with the most intense love, adore Him with the most fervent gratitude. Let us "praise Him according to His excellent greatness." (Ps. 150:2) Let us serve Him with all the strength of our capacity, with all the devotion of our will. Grace being a new principle added to our natural powers, as it directs our desires to a higher object, so it adds vigor to their activity. We shall best prove its dominion over us by seeking to exert ourselves in the spiritual cause with the same energy with which we once exerted ourselves in the cause of the world. The world was too little to fill our whole capacity. It is the glory of our Christian faith to supply One who is worthy of the entire consecration of every power, faculty and affection we have.

Chapter 8
Acknowledging the Hand of God in the Daily Circumstances of Life

If we would indeed love God, let us acquaint ourselves with Him. God has assured us in His Scriptures that there is no other way to be at peace. As we cannot love an unknown God, so neither can we know him, or even approach a knowledge of Him, except on the terms which He Himself holds out to us. Neither will He save us except by the method which He has Himself prescribed. His very perfections, those just objects of our adoration, all stand in the way of guilty creatures. His justice is the flaming sword which excludes us from the Paradise we have forfeited. His purity is so opposed to our corruptions, His wisdom to our follies, that were it not for His atoning sacrifice, those very attributes which are now our trust, would be our terror. The most opposite images of human conception are required to show us who God is to us in our natural state, and who He is to us after we become regenerate. The "consuming fire" is transformed into essential love. (Heb. 12:29)

As we cannot know the Almighty perfectly, so we cannot love Him with that pure flame which animates glorified spirits. But there is a preliminary acquaintance with Him, an initial love of Him, for which He has equipped us by His works, by His word, and by His Spirit. Even in this weak and barren soil some germs will shoot up, some blossoms will open. That celestial plant, when watered by the dews of heaven, and ripened by the Sun of Righteousness will, in a more friendly environment, expand into the fullness of perfection, and bear immortal fruits in the Paradise of God.

A cold and unemotional person, who longs after the fervent love of the supreme Being he sees in others, may take comfort if he finds a similar indifference in his worldly attachments. But if his affections are intense towards the perishable things of earth, while they are dead toward spiritual things, it is not because he is destitute of passions, but only that they are directed toward the wrong object. If however, he loves God with that measure of feeling with which God has endowed him, he will neither be punished nor rewarded for the fact that his stock is greater or smaller than that of his fellow creatures.

In those times when our sense of spiritual things is weak and low, we must not give way to distrust, but warm our hearts with the recollection of our better moments. Our motives to love are not now diminished, but when our spiritual frame is lower, our natural spirits are weaker. Where there is languor there will be discouragements. But we must press on. "Faint yet pursuing," must sometimes be the Christian's motto.

There is more merit (if ever we dare apply so arrogant a word to our worthless efforts), in persevering under depression and discomfort, than in the happiest flow of devotion when the tide of health and spirits runs high.

Where there is less gratification there is less interest. Our love may be equally pure though not equally fervent when we persist in serving our heavenly Father with the same constancy, though it may seem that He has withdrawn from us our familiar consolations. Perseverance may bring us to the very qualities the absence for which we have longing—"O tarry thou the Lord's leisure, be strong and He shall comfort thy heart." We are too ready to imagine that we are spiritual because we know something of religion. We appropriate to ourselves the pious sentiments we read, and we talk as if the thoughts of other men's heads were really the feeling of our own hearts. But piety is not rooted in the memory, but in the affections. The memory provides assistance in this, though it is a bad substitute. Instead of being elated when we meditate on some of the Psalmist's more beautiful passages, we should feel a deep self-abasement on the reflection, that even though our situation may sometimes resemble his, yet how unsuited to our hearts seem the ardent expressions of his repentance, the overflowing of his gratitude, the depth of his submission, the entireness of his self-dedication and the fervor of his love. But one who indeed can once say with him, "Thou art my portion," (Ps. 119:57) will, like him, surrender himself unreservedly to His service.

It is important that we never allow our faith, any more than our love, to be depressed or elevated by mistaking for its operations the ramblings of a busy imagination. Faith must not look for its character to erratic flights of fantasy. Once faith has fixed her foot on the immutable Rock of Ages, fastened her firm eye on the cross, and stretched out her triumphant hand to seize the promised crown, she will not allow her stability to depend on imagination's constant shiftings. She will not be driven to despair by the blackest shades of anxiety, nor be betrayed into a careless security by its most flattering and vivid allurements.

One cause for the fluctuations in our faith is that we are too ready to judge the Almighty as if He were one of us. We judge Him not by His own declarations of what He is and what He will do, but by our own low standards. Because we are too little disposed to forgive those who have offended us, therefore we conclude that God is not ready to pardon our offenses. We suspect Him of being implacable, because we are apt to be so. When we do forgive, it is usually grudgingly and superficially, therefore we infer that God will not forgive freely and fully. We make a hypocritical distinction between forgiving and forgetting injuries. God cleans the slate when He grants the pardon. He not only says, "thy sins and thy iniquities will I forgive," but "I will remember them no more." (Jer. 31:34)

We are disposed to emphasize the smallness of our offenses, as a plea for their forgiveness; whereas God, to exhibit the boundlessness of His own mercy, has taught us to enter a plea directly contrary to that: "Lord, pardon my guilt, for it is *great.*" (Ps. 25:11) To natural reason this argument of David is most extraordinary. But while he felt that the greatness of his own iniquity left him no human resource, he felt that God's mercy was greater even than his sin. What a large, what a magnificent picture this gives us of God's power and goodness, that, instead of pleading the smallness of our own offenses as a motive for pardon, we plead only the abundance of the divine compassion!

We are told that it is the duty of the Christian to "seek God." Yet it would be less repulsive to our corrupt nature to go on a pilgrimage to distant lands than to seek Him within our own hearts. Our own heart is truly an unknown territory, a land more foreign to us than the regions of the polar circle. Yet that heart is the place in which we must seek an acquaintance with God. It is there we must worship Him, if we would worship Him in spirit and in truth.

But alas, the heart is not a home for a worldly man; it is scarcely a home for a Christian. If business and pleasure are our natural inclinations, the resulting emptiness, sloth and insensibility—too often worse than the inclinations themselves, disqualify too many Christians and make them unwilling to pursue spiritual things.

I have observed that a common beggar if overtaken by a shower of rain, would rather find shelter under the wall of a churchyard, than to enter through the open church door while divine services are going on. It is less annoying to him to be drenched with the storm, than to enjoy the convenience of a shelter and a seat, if he must enjoy them at the heavy price of listening to the sermon.

While we condemn the beggar, let us look into our own hearts; can we not detect some of the same indolence, reticence, and distaste for serious things? Do we not find that we sometimes prefer our very pains, vexations and inconveniences to communing with our Maker? Happy are we if we would not rather be absorbed in our petty cares and little disturbances. We too often make them the means of occupying our minds and of drawing them away from that devout fellowship with God which demands the liveliest exercise of our rational powers, and the highest elevation of our spiritual affections. It should be easily understood that the dread of being driven to this sacred fellowship is a chief cause of that activity and restlessness which sets the world in such perpetual motion.

Though we are ready to express our general confidence in God's goodness, what practical evidences can we produce to prove that we really do trust Him? Does this trust deliver us from worldly anxiety? Does it free us from the same agitation of spirits which those who make no such profession endure? Does it relieve the mind of doubt and distrust? Does it fortify us against temptations? Does it produce in us "that work of righteousness which is peace," that effect of righteousness which is "quietness and assurance for ever"? (Isa. 32:17) Do we commit ourselves and our concerns to God in word, or in reality? Does this implicit reliance simplify our desires? Does it induce us to credit the testimony of His word and the promises of His Gospel? Do we not entertain some secret suspicions of His faithfulness and truth in our hearts when we persuade others in an attempt to persuade ourselves that we unreservedly trust Him?

In the preceding chapter we endeavored to illustrate how our lack of love for God is exposed when we are slower to *vindicate* the divine conduct than to justify the action of a mere human acquaintance. The same illustration may express our reluctance to *trust* in God. If a trusted friend does us a kindness, though he may not think it necessary to explain the particular manner in which he intends to do it, we take him at his word. Assured of the result, we are neither inquisitive about the mode nor the details. But do we treat our Almighty Friend with the same liberal confidence? Do we not murmur because we do not know where He is leading us and cannot follow His movements step by step? Do we wait for the development of His plan in full assurance that the results will be ultimately good? Do we trust that He is abundantly able to do more for us than we can ask or think, if by our suspicions we do not offend Him, and if by our infidelity we do not provoke Him? In short, do we not think ourselves utterly undone, when we have only Providence to trust in?

We are ready to acknowledge God in His mercies, nay, we confess Him in the daily enjoyments of life. In some of these common mercies, such as a bright day, a refreshing shower, or delightful scene, we discover that an excitement of spirits, a sort of carnal enjoyment, though of a refined nature, mixes itself with our devotional feelings; and though we confess and adore the bountiful Giver, we do it with a little mixture of self-complacency and human gratification. Fortunately He pardons and accepts us for this mixture.

But we must also look for Him in scenes less animating; we must acknowledge Him on occasions less exhilarating, less gratifying to our senses. It is not only in His promises that God manifests His mercy. His threatenings are proofs of the same compassionate love. His warnings are intended to snatch us from punishment.

We may also trace His hand not only in the awesome visitations of life, not only in the severer dispensations of His providence, but in vexations so trivial that we should hesitate to recognize that they are providential appointments, if we did not know that our daily life is made up of unimportant circumstances rather than of great events. As they are of sufficient importance to exercise the Christian desires and affections, we may trace the hand of our Heavenly Father in those daily little disappointments, the hourly vexations which occur even in the most prosperous circumstances, and which are inseparable from the condition of humanity. We must trace that same beneficent hand, secretly at work for our purification and our correction, in the imperfections and unpleasantness of those around us, in the perverseness of those with whom we transact business, and in those interruptions which break in upon our favorite engagements.

We are perhaps too much addicted to our innocent delights, or we are too fond of our leisure, our learning or even of our religious devotion. But while we say with Peter, "It is good for us to be here," (Matt. 17:4) the divine vision is withdrawn, and we are compelled to come down from the mount. Or perhaps we do not use our time of prayer for the purposes for which it was granted, and to which we had resolved to devote it, and our time is broken in upon to make us more sensible of its value. Or we feel a self-satisfaction in our leisure, a pride in our books or of the good things we are intending to say or do. A check then becomes necessary, but it is given in a most imperceptible way. The hand that gives it is unseen, is unsuspected, yet it is the same gracious hand which directs the more important events of life. Some annoying interruption breaks in on our projected privacy and calls us to a sacrifice of our inclination, to a renunciation of our own will. These incessant tests of our temper, if well received, may be more salutary to the mind than the finest passage we had intended to read, or the sublimest sentiment we had fancied to write.

Instead of searching for great mortifications, as a certain class of pious writers recommends, let us cheerfully bear and diligently receive these smaller trials which God prepares for us. Submission to a cross which He inflicts, to a disappointment which He sends, to a contradiction of our self-love which He appoints, is a far better exercise than great penances of our own choosing. Perpetual conquests over impatience, ill temper and self-will, indicate a better spirit than any self-imposed mortifications. We may traverse oceans and scale mountains on uncommanded pilgrimages without pleasing God. We may please Him without any other exertion than by crossing our own will.

Perhaps you had been busying your imagination with some projected scheme, not only lawful, but laudable. The design was basically good, but the involvement of your own will might interfere and even taint the purity of your best intentions. Your motives were so mixed that it was difficult to separate them. Sudden sickness obstructed the design. You naturally lament the failure, not perceiving that however good the work might be for others, the sickness was better for yourself. An act of charity was in

your intention, but God saw that you should have required
the exercise of a more difficult virtue; that the humility
and resignation, the patience and contrition of a sick bed
were more necessary for you. He accepts your plan as
far as it was designed for His glory, but then He calls
you to other duties, which were more honoring for Him,
and of which the Master was the better judge. He sets
aside your work and orders you to wait, which may be
the more difficult part of your task. To the extent that
your motive was pure, you will receive the reward of your
unperformed charity, though not the gratification of the
performance. If it was not pure, you are rescued from
the danger attending a right action performed on a worldly
principle. You may be the better Christian, though one
good deed is subtracted from your catalogue.

By a life of activity and usefulness, you had perhaps
attracted the public esteem. The love of reputation begins
to mix itself with your better motives. You do not, it is
presumed, act entirely, or chiefly for human applause; but
you are too concerned about it. It is a delicious poison
which begins to infuse itself into your purest cup. You
acknowledge indeed the sublimity of higher motives, but
you begin to feel that the human incentive is necessary,
and your spirits would flag if it were withdrawn.

This yearning for praise would gradually tarnish the
purity of your best actions. He who sees your heart as
well as your works, mercifully snatches you from the perils
of prosperity. Malice in others is awakened. Your most
meritorious actions are ascribed to the most corrupt
motives. You are attacked just where your character is most
vulnerable. The enemies whom your success raised up,
are raised up by God, not to punish you but to save you.
We are far from suggesting that He can ever be the author
of evil; He does not excite or approve the attack, but He
uses your accusers as instruments of your purification. Your
fame was too dear to you. It is a costly sacrifice, but God

requires it. It must be offered up. You would gladly embrace another offering, but this is the offering He chooses. And while He graciously continues to employ you for His glory, He thus teaches you to renounce your own. He sends this trial as a test, by which you are to try yourself. He thus instructs you not to abandon your Christian exertions, but to elevate the principle which inspired them, to rid it from all impure mixtures.

By thus stripping away the most engaging duties of this dangerous delight, by infusing some drops of bitterness into our sweetest drink, He graciously compels us to return to Himself. By taking away the buttresses by which we are perpetually propping up our sagging self-images, they fall to the ground. We are, as it were, driven back to Him, who condescends to receive us, though He knows we would not have returned to Him if everything else had *not* failed us. He makes us feel our weakness, that we may resort to His strength. He makes us sensible of our hitherto unperceived sins, that we may take refuge in His everlasting compassion.

Chapter 9
Christian Requirements Apply to All

It is not unusual to see people ignore some of the most solemn demands of Scripture by acting as if they do not apply to *them*. They consider these demands as belonging to the first age of the Gospel and to the individuals to whom they were immediately addressed. Consequently, they say, the need to observe them does not apply to "hereditary Christians."

These exceptions are particularly made for some of the most important teachings so forcibly and repeatedly expressed in the Epistles. Such reasoners persuade themselves that it was only the Ephesians who were "dead in trespasses and sin." "It was only the Galatians," they say, who were told "not to fulfill the lusts of the flesh." It was only the Philippians who were "enemies of the cross of Christ." Since they know neither the Ephesians, Galatians or Philippians, they have little or nothing to do with the reproofs or threatenings which were originally directed to the converts among those people. They console themselves with the belief that it was only these pagans who "walked according to the course of this world," who were "strangers from the covenants of promise" and were "without God in the world." (Eph. 2:12)

But these self-satisfied critics would do well to learn that not only "circumcision nor uncircumcision availeth nothing," but neither does "baptism or no baptism" (I mean as a mere form). The need in both cases is "a new creature." (Gal. 6:15) An irreligious person who professes to be a Christian is as much "a stranger and foreigner" as is an unbeliever. He is no more "a fellow citizen of the saints and of the household of God" (Eph. 2:19) than a Colossian or Galatian was before the Gospel came to him.

Before their conversion, the persons to whom the apostles preached had no vices to which we are not also susceptible, but they certainly had difficulties afterwards from which we are happily exempt. There were indeed differences between them and us in external situations and local circumstances, and we should take these into account. We can recognize that the epistles were addressed to specific situations, but not exclusively so. The purpose of the Scriptures—the conversion and instruction of the whole world—were far beyond limitation to any one period. Yes, these first-century converts were called miraculously "out of darkness into the marvelous light of the Gospel." (I Pet. 2:9) Yes, they were changed from gross blindness to illumination. Yes, by embracing the new faith they were exposed to persecution, reproach and dishonor. They were a few who had to struggle against the world. The laws, principalities and powers which support our faith oppose theirs.[1] We cannot lose sight of these distinctions.

---

[1] We must remember that the author writes in 19th century England. The modern world offers less of the support of law and custom for the believer. —Ed.

We have inherited advantages they never knew.

But however the condition of the external state of the Church might differ, there can be no difference in the interior state of the individual Christian. On whatever high principles of devotedness to God and love to man they were called to act, we are called to act in precisely the same. It may be that their faith was called to more painful exertions, their self-denial to harder sacrifices and their renunciation of earthly things to severer trials. But this would naturally be the case. The first introduction of Christianity had to combat the pride, prejudices and enmity of corrupt human nature invested with worldly power. Those in power could not fail to perceive how much this new faith opposed itself to their corruptions and that it was introducing a spirit in direct and avowed hostility to the spirit of the world.

We can be deeply thankful that we experience the diminished difficulties of an established faith, but let us never forget that Christianity allows no diminishment of the quality or abatement in the spirit which constituted a Christian in the first ages of the Church.

Christianity is precisely the same religion now as it was when our Savior was on earth. The spirit of the world is exactly the same now as it was then. And if the most eminent of the apostles, under the guidance of inspiration, was given to lament their conflicts with their own corrupt nature (the power of temptation combining with their natural inclinations to evil), how can we expect that a weaker faith and slackened zeal will be accepted in *us*? Believers *then* were not called to a more elevated devotion, a higher degree of purity, deeper humility or greater virtue, patience and sincerity than we are called today. The promises are not limited to the period in which they were made, and the aid of the Spirit is not confined to those on whom He was first poured out. Peter expressly declared that the Holy Spirit was promised not only to them and their children, "but to all who are afar off, even to as many as the Lord our God shall call." (Acts 2:39)

If the same salvation is now offered as was offered at first, is it not obvious that it must be worked out in the same way? The Gospel retains the same authority in all ages. It maintains the same universality among all ranks. Christianity has no bylaws, no particular exemptions, no individual immunities. That there is no appropriate way for a prince or a philosopher to achieve his own salvation is probably one reason why greatness and wisdom have so often rejected it. But if rank cannot plead its privileges neither can genius claim its distinctions. Christianity does not owe its success to the arts of rhetoric or the reason of schools, because God intended by it to make "foolish the wisdom of the world." (1 Cor. 1:20) This actually explains why the disputers of this world have always been its enemies.

It would have been unworthy of the infinite God to have imparted a partial religion. There is but one gate and that a "strait one." There is but one way and that a "narrow one." (Matt. 7:13, 14) The Gospel enjoins the same principles of love and obedience on all of every condition. It offers the same aids under the same difficulties, the same supports under all trials, the same pardon to all penitents, the same Savior to all believers and the same rewards to all who "endure to the end." (Mark 13:13) The temptations of one condition and the trials of another may call for the exercise of different qualities for the performance of different duties, but the same personal holiness is commanded for all. External acts of virtue may be promoted by some circumstances and impeded by others, but the graces of inward godliness are of universal force and eternal obligation.

The universality of its requirements is one of Christianity's most distinguishing characteristics. In the pagan world it seemed sufficient that a few exalted spirits, a few fine geniuses should soar above the mass. But it was never expected that the mob of Rome or Athens should aspire to any religious feelings in common with Socrates or Epicletus.

The most incontrovertible proof that "the world did not know God through wisdom" (I Cor. 1:21) is furnished by ancient Greece. At the very time and in the very country in which knowledge and taste had attained their utmost perfection, when education had given laws to human intellect, atheism first assumed a shape and established itself into a school of philosophy. It was at the moment when the intellectual powers of Greece were carried to their highest pitch that it was settled as an infallible truth in this philosophy that *the senses were the highest natural light of mankind.* And it was in the most enlightened age of Rome that this atheistic philosophy was transplanted there.

It seems as if the most accomplished nations stood in the most pressing need of the light of revelation; for it was not to the dark corners of the earth that the apostles had their earliest missions. One of St Paul's first and noblest expositions of Christian truth was made before the most august assembly in the world, on the Areopagus in Athens—although it appears that only one person was converted. In Rome some of the apostle's earliest converts belonged to the Imperial Palace. It was to the metropolis of cultivated Italy, to the "regions of Achaia," to the opulent and luxurious city of Corinth, in preference to the barbarous countries of the uncivilized world that some of his first epistles are addressed.

Even natural religion was little understood by those who professed it. It was full of obscurity until viewed by the clear light of the Gospel. Not only did natural religion need to be clearly comprehended, but reason itself remained to be carried to its highest pitch in countries where revelation was professed. Natural religion could not see itself by its own light, reason could not extricate itself from the labyrinth of error and ignorance in which false religion had involved the world. Grace has raised nature. Revelation has given a lift to reason and taught her to despise the follies and corruptions which obscured her brightness. If nature is now delivered from darkness, it was the helping hand of revelation which raised her from the rubbish in which she lay buried.

Christianity has not only given us right conceptions of God, of His holiness, of the way in which He would be worshipped, it has really taught us the right use of reason. It has given us those principles of examining and appraising by which we are enabled to judge the absurdity of false religions. "For to what else can be ascribed," says Bishop Sherlock, "that in every nation that names the name of Christ, even reason and nature see and condemn the follies to which others are still, for want of the same help, held in subjection?"

Suppose, however, that Plato and others seem to have been taught of heaven, yet the point is that their philosophy made no provision for the common people. The millions were left to live without knowledge and to die without hope. For what knowledge or what hope could be acquired from their preposterous though amusing and elegant mythology?

But they provided no common principle of hope or fear, of faith or practice, no source of consolation, no bond of charity, no communion of everlasting interests, no equality between the wise and the ignorant, the master and the slave, the Greek and the barbarian.

A religion was needed which would apply to everyone. Christianity happily filled the common urgent need. It furnished an adequate answer to the universal distress.

Instead of perpetual but unexpiating sacrifices to appease imaginary deities, it presents "one oblation once offered, a full, perfect and sufficient sacrifice, oblation and satisfaction for the sins of the whole world."[2] It presents one consistent scheme of morals growing out of one uniform system of doctrines; one perfect rule of practice depending on one principle of faith. It offers grace for both. It encircles the whole sphere of duty with the broad and golden zone of charity, stamped with the inscription, "A new commandment I give unto you, that you love one another." (John 13:34)

Were this command uniformly observed, the whole frame of society would be cemented and consolidated into one indissoluble bond of universal brotherhood. This divinely enacted law is the seminal principle of justice, charity, patience, forbearance—in short, of all social virtue. That it does not produce these excellent effects is not owing to any defect in the principle, but in our corrupt nature which so reluctantly and imperfectly obeys it. If it were conscientiously adopted and substantially acted upon, if it were received in its true spirit and obeyed from the heart, human laws might be rescinded, courts of justice abolished and treatises of morality burnt. War would no longer be an art, nor military tactics a science. We should suffer long and be kind, and so far from "seeking that which is another's," we should not even seek our own.

But let not the soldier or the lawyer be alarmed. Their craft is not in danger! The world does not intend to act upon the divine principle which would injure their professions, and until this revolution actually takes place, our fortunes will not be secure without the exertions of the law, nor our lives without the protection of the military.

All the virtues have their appropriate place and rank in Scripture. They are introduced as individually beautiful,

---

[2]   From The Book of Common Prayer

and as organically connected. But perhaps no Christian grace was ever more beautifully described than charity. Her incomparable painter, St Paul, has drawn her at full length in all her fair proportions. Every attitude is full of grace, every feature full of beauty. The whole portrayal is perfect and entire, wanting nothing.

Who can look at this finished piece without blushing at our own lack of likeness to it? Perhaps a more frequent contemplation of this exquisite figure, accompanied with earnest endeavor to become more like it, would gradually lead us, not simply to admire the picture, but would at length incorporate us into the divine original.

Chapter 10
Christian Holiness

Christianity, as we have attempted to show, calls for the same standards of goodness in different stations and in every person. No one can be allowed to rest in moral laxity and plead his exemption for aiming higher.

Those who keep its standards in their eye, though they may not reach the highest attainments, will not be satisfied with such as are unworthy. The obvious inferiority will produce compunction; compunction will stimulate them to press on. Those who lose sight of their standard, however, will be satisfied with the height they have already reached. They are not likely to be the object of God's favor who take their determined stand on the very lowest step in the scale of perfection, who do not even aspire above it, whose aim seems to be not so much to please God as to escape punishment. Many people will doubtless be accepted, though their progress has been small. Their difficulties may have been great, their natural capacity weak; their temptations were strong, and their instruction may have been defective.

Revelation has furnished injunctions as well as motives

to holiness; not only motives, but examples. "Be ye therefore perfect" (according to your measure and degree) "as your Father which is in heaven is perfect." (Matt. 5:48) And what says the Old Testament? It accords with the New: "Be ye holy, for I the Lord your God am holy." (Lev. 19:2)

This was the injunction of God himself, not given exclusively to Moses, the leader and legislator, or to a few distinguished officers, but to an immense body of people, even to the whole assembled host of Israel; to men of all ranks, professions, capacities, and characters, to the ministers of religion and the uninstructed, to enlightened rulers, and to feeble women. "God," says an excellent writer, "had already given to his people particular laws suited to their different needs and various conditions, but the command to be holy was a general (or universal) law."

"Who is like unto Thee, O Lord, among the gods? Who is like unto Thee, glorious in holiness, fearful in praises, doing wonders?" (Ex. 15:11) This is perhaps the sublimest praise addressed to God which the Scriptures have recorded. The term "holy" is more frequently affixed to the name of God than to any other. It has been remarked that the great blasphemy of the Assyrian monarch, Sennacherib, is not focused on his hostility against the Almighty God, but his crime is aggravated because he had committed it against *the Holy One of Israel.* (II Kings 19:22)

When God condescended to give a pledge for the performance of His promise, He swears by His holiness, as if it was the distinguishing quality which was more especially binding. It seems connected and interwoven with all the divine perfections. Which of His excellences can we contemplate as separated from this? Is not His justice stamped with sanctity? It is free from any tincture of vindictiveness, and is therefore a *holy* justice. His mercy has none of the partiality or favoritism, or capricious fondness of human kindness, but is a *holy* mercy. His holiness is not more the source of His mercies than of His punishments. If His holiness in His severities to us needed a justification, there cannot be a more substantial illustration of it than the passage already quoted. For God is called "glorious in holiness" immediately after He had vindicated the honor of His name by the miraculous destruction of the army of Pharaoh.

Does it not follow "That a righteous Lord loveth righteousness," (Ps. 11:7) and that He will require in His creatures a desire to imitate as well as to adore that attribute by which He Himself wills to be distinguished? We cannot indeed, like God, be essentially holy. God is the essence of holiness, and we can have no holiness nor any other good thing unless we derive it from Him. It is His by nature, but our privilege.

If God loves holiness because it is His image, He must consequently hate sin because it defaces His image. If He glorifies His own mercy and goodness in rewarding virtue, He no less vindicates the honor of His holiness in the punishment of vice. A perfect God can no more approve of sin in His creatures than He can commit it Himself. He may forgive sin on His own conditions, but there are no conditions on which He can be reconciled to it. The infinite goodness of God may delight in the beneficial purposes to which His infinite wisdom has made the sins of His creatures to serve, but sin itself will always be abhorrent to His nature. His wisdom may turn it to a merciful end, but His indignation at the offence cannot be diminished. He loves humankind, for He cannot but love His own work. He hates sin for that was man's own invention, and no part of the work which God had made. Even in the imperfect administration of human laws, impunity of crimes would be construed into approval of them.

The law of holiness then, is a law binding in all persons

without distinction, not limited to the period nor to the people to whom it was given. It reached through the whole Old Testament period, and extends with wider demands and higher sanctions, to every Christian of every denomination, of every age and every country.

A more sublime motive cannot be found as to why we should be holy than because "the Lord our God is holy." Men of the world have no objection to the terms virtue, morality, integrity, rectitude, but they associate something hypocritical with the term "holiness," and neither use it in a good sense when applied to others, nor would wish to have it applied to themselves, but apply it with a little suspicion, and not a little derision, to Puritans and "enthusiasts."[1]

This epithet however is surely rescued from every injurious association if we consider it as the chosen attribute of the Most High. We do not presume to apply the terms virtue, honesty and morality to God, but we ascribe holiness to Him because He first ascribed it to Himself, as the consummation of all His perfections.

Shall so imperfect a being as man then, ridicule the application of this term to others, or be ashamed of it himself? There is a reason indeed which should make him ashamed of the appropriation: that of not deserving it. This comprehensive appellation includes all the Christian graces, all the virtues in their just proportion, order, and harmony. And as in God, glory and holiness are united, so the Apostle combines "sanctification and honor" as the glory of man.

Traces of the holiness of God may be found in His works, to those who view them with the eye of faith. They

---

[1] In the 18th and 19th centuries the term "enthusiasm" was widely used for extravagance in religious devotion.

are more plainly visible in His providences; but it is in His Word that we must chiefly look for the manifestations of His holiness. He is everywhere described as perfectly holy in Himself, as a Model to be imitated by His creatures.

The doctrine of redemption is inseparably connected with the doctrine of sanctification. As one writer has observed, "If the blood of Christ reconciles us to the justice of God, the Spirit of Christ is to reconcile us to the holiness of God." When we are told therefore that Christ is made unto us "righteousness," we are in the same place taught that He is made unto us "sanctification" (I Cor. 1:30); that is, He is both Justifier and Sanctifier. In vain shall we deceive ourselves by resting on His sacrifice, while we neglect to imitate His example.

The glorious spirits which surround the throne of God are not represented as singing Hallelujahs to His omnipotence, nor even to His mercy, but they perpetually cry "Holy, holy, holy, Lord God of Hosts." (Isa. 6:3) It is significant, too, that the angels who adore Him for His holiness are the ministers of His justice.

This infinitely blessed Being then, to whom angels and archangels, and all the hosts of heaven are continually ascribing holiness, has commanded us to be holy. To be holy because God is holy, is both an argument and a command: an argument founded on the perfections of God, and a command to imitate Him. This command is given to creatures, fallen indeed, but to whom God graciously promises strength for the imitation. If in God holiness implies an aggregate of perfection, in humanity, even in our low degree, it is an incorporation of the Christian graces.

The holiness of God indeed is not limited; ours is bounded, finite, imperfect. Yet let us dare to extend our little sphere. Let our desires be large, though our capacities are small. Let our aims be lofty, though our attainments are low. Let us be careful to see that no day pass without

some increase in our holiness, some added height in our
aspiration, some wider expansion in the compass of our
virtues. Let us strive every day for some superiority to the
preceding day, something that shall distinctly mark the
passing scene with progress; something that shall inspire
an humble hope that we are less unfit for heaven today
than we were yesterday. The celebrated artist who has
recorded that he passed no day without drawing a line,
drew it not for repetition, but for progress; not to produce
a given number of strokes, but to forward his work, to
complete his design. The Christian, like the painter, does
not draw his lines at random. We have a Model to imitate
as well as an outline to fill. Every touch conforms us more
and more to the great Original. He who has transfused
most of the life of God into his soul has copied it most
successfully.

"To *seek* happiness," says one of the Fathers, "is to
desire God, and to find Him *in* that happiness." Our very
happiness therefore is not our independent possession.
It flows from that eternal Mind which is the Source and
Sum of happiness. In vain we look for felicity in all around
us. It can only be found in that original fountain, whence
we and all we are and have, are derived. Where then
is the imaginary wise man of the school of Zeno? What
is the perfection of virtue supposed by Aristotle? They
have no existence but in the romance of philosophy.
Happiness must be imperfect in an imperfect state. Our
Christian faith is introductory happiness, and points to
its perfection; but as the best persons possess it but
imperfectly, they cannot be perfectly happy. Nothing can
confer completeness which is itself incomplete. "With
Thee, O Lord, is the fountain of life, and in Thy light
only we shall see light." (Ps. 36:9)

Whatever shall still remain lacking in our attainments,
and much will still remain, let this last, greatest, highest
consideration stimulate our faint exertions, that God has

negatively promised the beatific vision, the enjoyment of His presence, to this attainment, by specifically proclaiming that without holiness no man shall see His face. To know God is the foundation of that eternal life which will hereafter be perfected by seeing Him. As there is no stronger reason why we must not look for perfect happiness in this life than because there is no perfect holiness, so the nearer we advance toward holiness, the greater progress we shall make towards perfect happiness. We must cultivate those tendencies and tempers here which must be carried to perfection in a happier place. But since holiness is the essential ingredient of happiness, so must it be its precursor. As sin has destroyed our happiness, so sin must be destroyed before our happiness can be restored. Our nature must be renovated before our felicity can be established. This is according to the nature of things as well as agreeable to the law and will of God. Let us then carefully look to the subduing in our inmost hearts all those dispositions that are unlike God, all those actions, thoughts and tendencies that are contrary to God.

Independently therefore of all the other motives to holiness which our faith suggests; independently of the fear of punishment, independently even of the hope of glory, let us be holy from this ennobling, elevating motive, because the Lord our God is holy. And when our virtue flags, let it be renewed by this imperative motive, backed by this irresistible argument. The motive for imitation, and the Being to be imitated seem almost to identify us with infinity. It is a connection which endears, an assimilation which dignifies, a resemblance which elevates. The apostle has added to the prophet an assurance which makes the crown and consummation of the promise, that though we know not yet what we shall be, "we shall be like Him, for we shall see Him as He is." (I Jn. 3:2)

In what a beautiful variety of glowing expressions, and admiring strains, do the Scripture worthies delight to represent God! They speak not only in relation to what He is to them, but to the supreme excellence of His own transcendent perfections. They that dwell with unwearied repetition on the adorable theme; they ransack language, they exhaust all the expressions of praise and wonder and admiration, all the images of astonishment and delight to laud and magnify His glorious name. They praise him, they bless Him, they worship Him, they glorify Him, they give thanks to Him for His great glory, saying, "Holy, holy, holy, Lord God of hosts, Heaven and earth are full of the majesty of Thy glory." (Isa. 6:3)

They glorify Him in relation to themselves."I will magnify Thee, O Lord my strength. My help cometh of God. The Lord Himself is the portion of my inheritance." (Pss. 18:1; 121:2; 16:5) At another time soaring with a noble disinterest and quite losing sight of self and all created glories, they adore Him for His excellencies. "Oh the depth of the riches both of the wisdom and knowledge of God!" (Rom. 11:33) Then bursting to a rapture of adoration, and burning with a more intense flame, they assemble His attributes: "To the King eternal, immortal, invisible, be honor and glory for ever and ever." (I Tim. 1:17) *One* is lost in admiration of His wisdom. His ascription is "to the only wise God." *Another* in triumphant strains overflows with transport at the consideration of the attribute of His holiness: "Lord, who is like unto Thee, there is none holy as the Lord. Sing praises unto the Lord, oh ye saints of His, and give thanks unto Him for a remembrance of His holiness." (Ps. 30:4)

The prophets and apostles were not deterred from pouring out the overflowings of their fervent spirits, they were not restrained from celebrating the perfections of their Creator through the fear of being called "Enthusiasts." The saints of old were not prevented from breathing out their rapturous Hosannas to the King of saints, through the cowardly dread of being branded as fanatics. The conceptions of their minds expanded with the view of the glorious constellation of the Divine attributes; and the affections of their hearts warmed with the thought that those attributes were all concentrated in mercy. They display a sublime oblivion of themselves, forgetting everything but God. Their own wants dwindle to a point. Their own concerns and the universe itself shrink into nothing. They seem absorbed in the dazzling brilliance of Deity, lost in the radiant beams of His infinite glory.

Chapter 11
On the Comparatively Small Faults and Virtues

The "Fishers of Men," as if exclusively bent on catching the greater sinners, often make the openings of the moral net so wide that it cannot retain sinners of more ordinary size which everywhere abound. Their catch might be more abundant, if the net were woven tighter so the smaller, slipperier sinner could not slide through. Such souls, having happily escaped entanglement, plunge back again into their native element, enjoy their escape, and hope for time to grow bigger before they are in danger of being caught.

It is important to practice the smaller virtues, to avoid scrupulously the lesser sins, and to bear patiently with minor trials. The sin of always yielding tends to produce debility of mind which brings defeat, while the grace of always resisting in comparatively small points tends to produce that vigor of mind on which hangs victory.

Conscience is moral discernment. It quickly perceives good and evil and prompts the mind to adopt the one or avoid the other. God has furnished the body with senses, and the soul with conscience, an instinct to avoid the approach of danger and a spontaneous reaction to any attack whose suddenness and surprise allows no time for thoughtful consideration. If kept tenderly alive by paying continual attention to its admonitions, an enlightened conscience would especially preserve us from those smaller sins, and stimulate us to those lesser duties which we are falsely apt to overlook. We are prone to think they are too insignificant to be judged in the court of faith or too trivial to be weighed by the standard of Scripture.

By cherishing this quick sense of rectitude—this sudden flash from heaven, which is in fact the motion of the Spirit—we intuitively reject what is wrong before we have time to examine why it is wrong, and seize on what is right before we have time to examine why it is right. Should we not then be careful how we extinguish this sacred spark? Will anything be more likely to extinguish it than to neglect its hourly reminders to perform the smaller duties? Will anything more effectively smother it than to ignore the lesser faults, which make up a large part of human life, and will naturally fix and determine our character? Will not our neglect or observance of the voice of conscience incline or indispose us for those more important duties, of which these smaller ones are connecting links?

Vices derive their existence from wildness, confusion and disorganization. The discord of the passions is owing to their having different views, conflicting aims, and opposite ends. The rebellious vices have no common head. Each is all to itself. They promote their own operations by disturbing those of others, but in disturbing, they do not destroy them. Though they are all of one family, they live on no friendly terms. Extravagance hates covetousness as much as if it were a virtue. The life of every sin is a life of conflict which causes the torment, but not the death of its opposite sin.

On the other hand, without being united the Christian graces could not be perfected. The smaller virtues are the threads and filaments which gently but firmly tie them together. There is an attractive power in goodness which draws each part to the other. This harmony of the virtues is derived from their having one common center in which all meet. In vice there is a strong repulsion. Though bad men seek each other, they do not love each other. Each seeks the other in order to promote his own purposes, but at the same time he hates him.

Perhaps the beauty of the lesser virtues may be illustrated by gazing into the heavens at that long and luminous track of minute and almost imperceptible stars. Though separately they are too inconsiderable to attract attention, yet from their number and confluence they form that soft and shining stream of light which is everywhere discernible.

Every Christian should consider religion as a fort which he is called to defend. The lowest soldier in the army, if he add patriotism to valor, will fight as earnestly as if the glory of the whole contest depended on his single arm. But he brings his watchfulness as well as his courage into action. He strenuously defends every pass he is appointed to guard, without inquiring whether it be great or small. There is not any defect in religion or morals so little as to be of no consequence. Worldly things may be little because their aim and end may be little. Things are great or small, not according to their apparent importance, but according to the magnitude of their purpose and the importance of their consequences.

The acquisition of even the smallest virtue is actually a conquest over the opposite vice and doubles our moral strength. The spiritual enemy has one subject less, and the conqueror one virtue more.

By being negligent in small things, we are not aware how much we injure Christianity in the eyes of the world.

How can we expect people to believe that we are in earnest in great points when they see that we cannot withstand a trivial temptation? At a distance they hear with respect of our general characters. Then they get to know us and discover the same failings, littleness, and bad tempers as they have been accustomed to encounter in the most ordinary persons. Shall not the Christian be anxious to support the credit of his holy profession by not betraying in everyday life any temperament that is inconsistent with his faith?

It is not difficult to attract respect on great occasions, where we are kept faithful by knowing that the public eye is fixed upon us. Then it is easy to maintain our dignity, but to labor to maintain it in the seclusion of domestic privacy requires more watchfulness, and is no less a duty for the consistent Christian.

Our neglect of inferior duties is particularly injurious to the minds of our families. If they see us "weak and infirm of purpose," peevish, irresolute, capricious, passionate or inconsistent in our daily conduct, they will not give us credit for those higher qualities which we may possess and those superior duties which we may be more careful to fulfill. They may not see evidence by which to judge whether our thinking is true; but there will be obvious and decisive proofs of the state and temper of our hearts. Our greater qualities will do them little good, while our lesser but incessant faults do them much injury. Seeing us so defective in the daily course of our behavior at home, though our children may obey us because they are obliged to it, they will neither love nor esteem us enough to be influenced by our instruction or advice.

In all that relates to God and to himself, the Christian knows of no *small* faults. He considers sins, whatever their magnitude, as an offence against his Maker. Nothing that offends *Him* can be insignificant. Nothing can be trifling that makes a bad habit fasten itself to us. Faults which we are accustomed to consider as small are apt to be repeated without reservation. The habit of committing them is strengthened by the repetition. Frequency renders us at first indifferent, and then insensible. The hopelessness attending a long-indulged custom generates carelessness, until for lack of exercise, the power of resistance is first weakened, then destroyed.

But there is a still more serious point of view to consider. Do small faults, continually repeated, always retain their original weakness? Is a bad temper which is never repressed not worse after years of indulgence than when we first gave the reins to it? Does that which we first allowed ourselves under the name of harmless levity on serious subjects, never proceed to profaneness? Does what was once admired as proper spirit, never grow into pride, never swell into insolence? Does the habit of loose talking or allowed exaggeration never lead to falsehood, never move into deceit? Before we positively determine that small faults are innocent, we must try to prove that they shall never outgrow their primitive dimensions. We must make certain that the infant shall never become a giant.

For example, *procrastination* is reckoned among the most excusable of our faults, and weighs so lightly on our minds that we scarcely apologize for it. But, what if, from mere sloth and indolence, we had put off giving assistance to one friend under distress, or advice to another under temptation. Can we be sure that had we not delayed we might have preserved the well-being of the one, or saved the soul of the other?

It is not enough that we perform duties; we must perform them at the right time. We must do the duty of every day in its own season. Every day has it own demanding duties; we must not depend upon today for fulfilling those which we neglected yesterday, for today might not have been granted to us. Tomorrow will be equally demanding with its own duties; and the succeeding day, if we live to see it, will be ready with its proper claims.

Indecision, though it is not so often caused by reflection as by the lack of it, may be just as mischievous, for if we spend too much time in balancing probabilities, the period for action is lost. While we are busily considering difficulties which may never occur, reconciling differences which perhaps do not exist, and trying to balance things of nearly the same weight, the opportunity is lost for producing that good which a firm and bold decision would have effected.

Idleness, though itself the most inactive of all the vices, is however the path by which they all enter, the stage on which they all act. Though supremely passive itself, it lends a willing hand to all evil. It aids and encourages every sin. If it does nothing itself, it connives all the mischief that is done by others.

Vanity is exceedingly misplaced when ranked with small faults. It is under the guise of harmlessness that it does all its mischief. Vanity is often found in the company of great virtues, and by mixing itself in it, mars the whole collection. The use our spiritual enemy makes of it is a master stroke. When he cannot prevent us from doing right actions he can accomplish his purpose almost as well by making us vain about them. When he cannot deprive others of our good works he can defeat the effect in us by poisoning our motive. When he cannot rob others of the good effect of the deed, he can gain his point by robbing the doer of his reward.

Irritability is another of the minor miseries. Life itself, though sufficiently unhappy, cannot devise misfortunes as often as the irritable person can supply impatience. Violence and belligerence are the common resource of those whose knowledge is small, and whose arguments are weak. Anger is the common refuge of insignificance.

People who feel their character to be slight, hope to give it weight by inflation. But the blown balloon at its fullest distension is still empty.

Trifling is ranked among the venial faults. But, consider that time is one grand gift given to us in order that we may secure eternal life. If we trifle away that time so as to lose that eternal life, then it will serve to fulfill the very aim of sin. A life devoted to trifles not only takes away the inclination, but the capacity for higher pursuits. The truths of Christianity scarcely have more influence on a frivolous than on a depraved character. If the mind is so absorbed not merely with what is vicious, but with what is useless, it loses all interest in a life of piety. It matters little what causes this lack of interest. If such a fault cannot be accused of being a great moral evil, it at least reveals a low state of mind that a being who has eternity at stake can abandon itself to trivial pursuits. If the great concern of life cannot be secured without habitual watchfulness, how is it to be secured by habitual carelessness? It will afford little comfort to the trifler when at the last reckoning he accuses the more ostensible offender of worse behavior. The trifler will not be weighed in the scale with the profligate, but in the balance of the sanctuary.

Some will rationalize and excuse their lesser faults. They may even determine at what period of their lives such vices may be adopted without discredit, at what age one bad habit may give way to another more in character. Having accepted it as a matter of course that to a certain age certain faults are neutral, they proceed to act as if they even thought them inevitable.

But let us not believe that any failing, much less any vice, is necessarily a part of any particular state or age, or that it is irresistible at any time. We may accustom ourselves to talk of vanity and extravagance as belonging to the young, and avarice and cantankerousness to the old, until the next step will be that we shall think ourselves justified in adopting them. Whoever is eager to find excuses for vice and folly will feel less able to resist them.

We make a final excuse for ourselves when we ask whether or not the evil is of a greater or lesser magnitude. If the fault is great, we lament our inability to resist it, and if small, we deny the importance of doing so. We plead that we cannot withstand a great temptation, and that a small one is not worth withstanding. We rationalize that if the temptation or the fault is great, we should resist it because of its very magnitude, and if it is small, giving it up can cost but little. The conscientious habit of conquering the lesser wrong, however, will give considerable strength towards subduing the greater.

Then there is the person who, winding himself up occasionally to certain shining actions, thinks himself fully justified in breaking loose from the shackles of restraint in smaller things. He is not ashamed to gain favor through good deeds, at the same time permitting himself indulgences which, though allowed, are far from innocent. He thus secures to himself praise and popularity by means that are sure to gain it, and immunity from rebuke as he indulges himself in his favorite fault, practically exclaiming, "Is it not a little one?"

Vanity is at the bottom of almost all, may we not say, of all our sins. We think more of distinguishing than of saving ourselves. We overlook the hourly occasions which occur for serving, aiding and comforting those around us, while we perform an act of well-known generosity. The habit in the former case, however, better shows the disposition and bent of the mind, than the solitary act of splendor. The apostle does not say whatsoever *great* things ye do, but "whatsoever things ye do, do *all* to the glory of God." (I Cor. 10:31) Actions are less weighed by their bulk than their motive. The racer proceeds in his course more effectively by a steady unslackened pace, than by starts of violent but unequal effort.

That great moral law, of which we have elsewhere spoken [Chapter 9], that rule of the highest court of appeal, to which every man can always resort is this: "All things that ye would that men should do unto you, do ye also unto them." This law, if faithfully obeyed, would be an infallible remedy for all the disorders of self-love, and would establish the exercise of all the smaller virtues. Its strict observance would not only put a stop to all injustice, but to all unkindness; not only to oppressive acts, but to cruel speech. Even haughty looks and arrogant gestures would be banished from the face of society if we asked ourselves how we should like to receive what we are not ashamed to give.

Until we thus morally trade place, person, and circumstance with those of our brother, we shall never treat him with the tenderness this gracious law enjoins. To treat a fellow creature with harsh language is not indeed a crime like robbing him of his estate or destroying his reputation. They are, however, all the offspring of the same family. They are the same in quality, though not in degree. All flow from the same fountain, though in streams of different magnitude. All are indications of a departure from that principle which is included in the law of love.

The reason those called "religious people" often differ so little from others in small trials is that instead of bringing religion to their aid in their lesser vexations, they either allow the disturbances to prey upon their minds, or they look to the wrong things for their removal. Those who are rendered unhappy by frivolous troubles, seek comfort in frivolous enjoyments. But we should apply the same remedy to ordinary trials as to great ones. For just as small anxieties spring from the same cause as great trials—

namely, the uncertain and imperfect condition of human life—so they require the same remedy. Meeting common cares with a right spirit would impart a smoothness to the temper, a spirit of cheerfulness to the heart which would mightily break the force of heavier trials.

You seek help in your faith in dealing with great evils. Why does it not occur to you to seek it in the less? Is it that you think the instrument greater than the occasion demands? You would exercise your faith at the loss of your child, so exercise it at the loss of your temper. As no calamity is too great for the power of Christianity to mitigate, so none is too small to experience His beneficial results. Our behavior under the ordinary accidents of life forms a characteristic distinction between different classes of Christians. Those least advanced resort to religion on great occasions. What makes it appear of so little comparative value is that the medicine prepared by the great Physician is discarded instead of being taken. The patient does not use it except in extreme cases. A remedy, however potent, if not applied, can bring no healing. But he who has adopted one fixed rule for the government of his life, will try to keep the remedy in perpetual use.

Mundane duties are not great in themselves, but they become important by being constantly demanded. They make up in frequency what they lack in magnitude. How few of us are called to carry the doctrines of Christianity into distant lands, but which of us is not called every day to adorn those doctrines by gentleness in our own bearing, by kindness and patience to all about us?

Vanity provides no motive for performing unseen duties. No love of fame inspires that virtue of which fame will never hear. There can be but one motive, and that the purest, for the exercise of virtues when the report of them will never reach beyond the little circle whose happiness they promote. They do not fill the world with our renown, but they fill our own family with comfort. And if they have the love of God for their motive, they will have His favor for their reward.

What we refer to here are habitual and unresisted faults: habitual, because they go by unresisted, and allowed because they are considered to be too insignificant to call for resistance. Faults into which we fall inadvertently, though that is no reason for committing them, may not be without their uses. When we see them for what they are they renew the conviction of our own sinful nature, make us little in our own eyes, increase our sense of dependence on God, promote watchfulness, deepen humility, and quicken repentance.

We must, however, be careful not to entangle our consciences with groundless apprehensions. We have a merciful Father, not a hard master to deal with. We must not harass our minds with a suspicious dread, as if the Almighty were laying snares to entrap us. Nor should we be terrified with imaginary fears, as if He were on the watch to punish every casual error. Being immutable and impeccable is not part of human nature. He who made us best knows of what we are made. Our compassionate High Priest will bear with much infirmity and will pardon much involuntary weakness.

But every man who looks into his own heart must know the difficulties he has in serving God faithfully. Yet, though he earnestly desires to serve Him, it is lamentable that he is not more attentive to remove all that hinders him by trying to avoid the inferior sins, resisting the lesser temptations, and by practicing the smaller virtues. The neglect of these obstructs his way, and keeps him back in the performance of higher duties. Instead of little renunciations being grievous, and slight self-denials being hardship, they in reality soften grievances and diminish hardship. They are the private drill which trains us for public service.

We are hourly furnished with occasions for showing

our piety by the spirit in which the quiet, unobserved actions of life are performed. The sacrifices may be too little to be observed except by him to whom they are offered. But small services, scarcely perceptible to any eye but his for whom they are made, bear the true character of love to God, as they are the infallible marks of charity to our fellow creatures.

By enjoining small duties, the spirit of which is everywhere implied in the Gospel, God's intention seems to be to make the great ones easier for us. He makes the light yoke of Christ still lighter, not by lessening duty, but by increasing its ease through its familiarity. These little habits at once indicate the sentiment of the soul and improve it.

It is an awsome consideration, and one which every Christian should bring home to our own bosoms, whether or not small faults willfully persisted in, may in time not only dim the light of conscience, but extinguish the spirit of grace. Will indulgence in small faults ultimately dissolve all power of resistance against great evils? We should earnestly seek to remember that perhaps among the first objects which may meet our eyes when we open them on the eternal world, may be a tremendous book. In that book, together with our great and actual sins, may be recorded in no less prominent characters, an ample page of omissions and of neglected opportunities. There we may read a list of those good intentions, which indolence, indecision, thoughtlessness, vanity, trifling, and procrastination served to frustrate and to prevent.

Chapter 12

Self-Examination

In this age of exploration every kind of ignorance is regarded as dishonorable. In almost every sort of knowledge there is a competition for superiority. It is true that intellectual attainments are never to be undervalued. All knowledge is excellent as far as it goes, and as long as it lasts. But how short the period is before "tongues will cease, and knowledge will pass away!" (I Cor. 13:8)

Shall we then regard it as dishonorable to be ignorant in anything which relates to life and literature, to taste and science, and not feel ashamed to live in ignorance of our own hearts?

To have a flourishing estate, but a mind in disorder; to keep exact accounts with others, but no reckoning with our Maker; to have an accurate knowledge of profit or loss in our business, but to remain utterly ignorant as to whether our spiritual state is improving or declining; to calculate at the end of every year how much we have increased or diminished our fortune, but to be careless whether we have gained or lost in faith and holiness— this is a grievous miscalculation of the comparative value of things. To pay attention to things in an inverse proportion to their importance is surely proof that our learning has not improved our judgment.

The distinguishing faculty of self-inspection would not have been given us if it had not been intended that we should use it regularly. It is surely just as sensible to look well to our spiritual as to our worldly possessions. We have appetites to control, imaginations to restrain, tempers to regulate, passions to subdue, and how can this internal work be done, how can our thoughts be kept within proper bounds, how can appropriate direction be given to our affections, how can our inward state be preserved from continual insurrection if we do not exercise this capacity to inspect ourselves? Without constant discipline, imagination will become an outlaw and conscience a rebel.

This inward eye is given to us for a continual watch upon the soul. Both the formation and the growth of our moral and religious character depends upon a constant vigilance over the soul's interior movements. A sporadic glance is not enough for a thing so deep. An unsteady view will not suffice for a thing so wavering, nor a casual look for a thing so deceitful as the human heart. Such an object must be observed under a variety of aspects, because it is always shifting its position, always changing its appearances.

We should examine not only our conduct but our opinions. Our actions themselves will be obvious enough. It is our inward motivations which require the scrutiny. These we should follow to their remotest springs, scrutinize to their deepest recesses, trace through their most perplexing windings. And lest we should in our pursuit wander in uncertainty and blindness, let us make use of that guiding clue which the Almighty has furnished by His Word and by His Spirit. He will conduct us through the intricacies of this labyrinth. "What I know not, teach

Thou me" (Job 34:32) should be our constant petition in all our researches.

If we would turn our thoughts inward we would abate much of the self-complacency with which we swallow the flattery of others. If we would examine our motives keenly, we would frequently blush at the praises our actions receive. Let us then conscientiously enquire not only what we do, but why we do it.

Self-inspection is the only means to preserve us from self-conceit. Self-acquaintance will give us a far more deep and intimate knowledge of our own errors than we can possibly have by curiously inquiring into the errors of others. We are eager enough to blame them without knowing their motives. We are just as eager to vindicate ourselves, though we cannot be entirely ignorant of our own. Thus two virtues will be acquired by the same act of self-examination: humility and candor. An impartial review of our own infirmities is the likeliest way to make us tender and compassionate to those of others.

We shall not be liable to overrate our own judgment when we perceive that it often forms such false estimates. It is so captivated with trifles, so elated with petty successes, so dejected with little disappointments, that when others commend our charity, which we know is so cold, when others extol our piety, which we feel to be so dead, when they applaud the strength of our faith, which we know to be so faint and feeble, we cannot possibly be intoxicated with the applause which never would have been given had the applauder known us as we know, or ought to know ourselves. If we contradict him, it may only be to have a further virtue attributed to us—humility, which perhaps we deserve to have ascribed to us as little as those which we have been renouncing. If we kept a sharp lookout we would not be proud of praises which cannot apply to us, but would rather grieve at the fraud we commit by tacitly accepting a character to which we have so little real pretension. To be delighted at finding that people think so much better of us than we are conscious of deserving is in effect to rejoice in the success of our own deceit.

We shall also become more patient, more forbearing and forgiving, and shall better endure the harsh judgment of others when we perceive that their opinion of us nearly coincides with our own real, though unacknowledged, sentiments. There is much less injury incurred by others thinking too ill of us than in our thinking too well of ourselves.

It is evident then, that to live *at random,* is not the life of a rational, much less an immortal, least of all an accountable being. To pray occasionally, without a deliberate course of prayer, to be liberal without a plan, and charitable without a motive, to let the mind float on the current of public opinion, to be every hour liable to death without any habitual preparation for it, to carry within us a soul which we believe will exist through all the countless ages of eternity, and yet to make little enquiry whether that eternity is likely to be happy or miserable— all this is totally thoughtless. If adopted in the ordinary concerns of life, such a way to live would ruin a man's reputation for common sense. Yet he who lives without self-examination is absolutely guilty of this folly.

Nothing more plainly shows us what weak, vacillating creatures we are than the difficulty we find in holding ourselves to the very self-scrutiny we had deliberately resolved on. Some trifle which we should be ashamed to dwell upon at any time intrudes itself on the moments dedicated to serious thought. Recollection is interrupted. The whole chain of reflection is broken so that the scattered links cannot again be united. And so inconsistent are we that we are sometimes not sorry to have a plausible pretense for interrupting the very employment to which we had just committed ourselves. For lack of this inward acquaintance, we remain in utter ignorance of our inability to meet even the ordinary trials of life with cheerfulness. Nursed in the lap of luxury, we have no notion that we have but a loose hold on the things of this world, and of the world itself. But let some accident take away not the world, but some trifle on which we thought we set no value while we possessed it, we find to our astonishment that we hold, not the world only, but even this trivial possession with a pretty tight grasp. Such detections of our self-ignorance ought at least to humble us.

There is a spurious sort of self-examination which does not serve to enlighten but to blind. People who have given up some notorious vice, who have softened some shades of a glaring sin, or substituted some outward forms in the place of open irreligion, may look on their change of character with pleasure. They compare themselves with what they were and view the alteration with self-complacency. They deceive themselves by taking their standard from their former conduct, or from the character of others who are worse, instead of taking it from the unerring rule of Scripture. He looks more at the discredit than the sinfulness of his former life. Being more ashamed of what is disreputable than grieved at what is vicious, he is, in this state of shallow reformation, more in danger in proportion as he gives himself more credit. He is not aware that having a fault or two less will not carry him to heaven while his heart is still glued to the world and estranged from God.

If we ever look into our hearts at all, we are naturally most inclined to it when we think we have been acting right. In this case, self-inspection gratifies self-love. We have no great difficulty in directing our attention to an object when that object presents us with pleasing images.

But it is a painful effort to compel the mind to turn in on itself when the view only presents subjects for regret and remorse. This painful duty however must be performed, and will bring more healing in proportion as it is less pleasant. Let us establish it into a habit to ponder our faults. We need not feed our vanity with the recollection of our virtues. They will, if that vanity does not obliterate them, be recorded elsewhere.

We are also most disposed to look at those parts of our character which will best bear it, and which consequently least need it; at those parts which afford most self-gratification. If a covetous man, for instance, examines himself, instead of turning his attention to the guilty part, he applies the probe where he knows it will not go very deep; he turns from his greed to that abstention of which his very avarice is perhaps the source. Another, who is the slave of passion, fondly rests upon some act of generosity, which he considers as a fair exchange for some favorite vice that would cost him more to renounce than he is willing to part with. We are all too much disposed to dwell on that smiling side of the view which pleases and deceives us, and to shut our eyes upon that part which we do not choose to see, because we are resolved not to stop. Self-love always holds a screen between the superficial self-examiner and his faults. The nominal Christian wraps himself up in forms which he makes himself believe are religion. He exults in what he does, overlooks what he ought to do and never suspects that what is done at all can be done amiss.

We are usually so indolent that we seldom examine a truth on more than one side, so we generally take care that it shall be that side which shall confirm some old prejudices. We will not take pains to correct those prejudices and to rectify our judgment, lest it should oblige us to discard a favorite opinion. We are still as eager to judge and as presumptuous to decide as if we fully possessed the grounds on which a sound judgment may be made, and a just decision formed.

We should watch ourselves whether we observe a simple rule of truth and justice in our conversations as well as in our ordinary transactions. Are we exact in our measures of commendation and censure? Do we not bestow extravagant praise where simple approval alone is due? Do we not withhold commendation, where if given, it would support modesty and encourage merit? Do we reprimand as immoral what deserves only a slight censure as imprudent? Do we not sometimes pretend to overrate ordinary merit in the hope of securing to ourselves the reputation of candor, so that we may on other occasions, with less suspicion, depreciate established excellence? We may be extolling ordinary merit because we think that it can come into no competition with us, and we denigrate excellence because it obviously eclipses us.

It is only by scrutinizing the heart that we can know it. Any careless observer may see that his watch has stopped by casting an eye on its face, but it is only the expert who takes it to pieces and examines every spring and every wheel separately. By ascertaining the precise cause of the problem he sets the watch right and restores the hidden movements.

The illusions of intellectual vision would be corrected by a close habit of cultivating an acquaintance with our hearts. We fill much too large a space in our own imaginations and fancy that we take more room in the world than Providence assigns to an individual who has to divide his allotment with so many millions who are all of equal importance in their own eyes. The conscientious practice we have been recommending would greatly assist in reducing us to our proper dimensions and limiting us to our proper place. We should be astonished if we could see our real smallness and the speck we actually occupy. When shall we learn from our own feelings how much consequence every person is to himself or herself?

Self-examination must not be occasional, but regular. Let us settle our accounts frequently. Little articles will run up to a large amount if they are not cleared off. Even our *innocent* days, as we may choose to call them, will not have passed without furnishing their measure of faults. Our deadness in devotion, our eagerness for human applause, our care to conceal our faults rather than to correct them, our negligent performance of some relative duty, our imprudence in conversation, especially at table, our inconsideration, driving to the very edge of permitted indulgences—let us keep all our numerous items in small sums. We can examine them while the particulars are fresh in our memory. Otherwise, we may find when we come to settle the grand account that these faults have not been forgotten.

And let one subject of our frequent inquiry be to ask whether, since we last examined our hearts, our secular affairs or our eternal concerns have had the predominance. We do not mean which of them occupied most of our time. Naturally, the larger portion must necessarily be absorbed in the cares of the present life. What we need to ask is how have we conducted ourselves when a competition arose between the interests of both.

That general burst of sins which so frequently rushes in on the consciences of the dying would be much moderated by previous habitual self-examination. The sorrow must be as precise as the sin. Indefinite repentance is no repentance. And it is one helpful use of self-enquiry to remind us that all unforsaken sins are unrepented sins.

To a Christian there is this substantial comfort which follows minute self-inspection: when we find fewer sins to be noted and more victories over temptations obtained, we have solid evidence of our advancement which well repays our trouble.

The faithful searcher into his own heart feels himself

in the situation of Ezekiel, who being conducted in vision from one idol to another, the spirit at sight of each repeatedly exclaims, "Here is another abomination!" The prophet was commanded to dig deeper, and the further he penetrated, the more evils he found, while the spirit continued to cry out, "I will show you yet more abominations." (Ezek. 8:6)

Self-examination, by detecting self-love, self-denial by weakening its powers and self-government by reducing its tyranny, turns the disposition of the soul from its natural bias, controls the disorderly appetite, and under the influence of divine grace restores to the person the dominion over himself that God first gave us over the lower creatures. Desires, passions and appetites are brought to move somewhat more in their appointed order—as subjects, not tyrants. In the end, self-examination restores us to dominion over our own will, and in good measure enthrones us in that empire which we forfeited by sin.

We now begin to survey our interior, the awful world within, not with complacency but with the control of a Sovereign, and we still find too much rebellion to feel ourselves secure. Therefore we continue our inspection with vigilance but without agitation. We continue to experience a remainder of insubordination and disorder, but this calls forth a stricter supervision rather than driving us to relax our discipline.

This self-inspection somewhat resembles the correction of a literary effort. After many careful revisions, though some grosser faults may be removed, though the errors are neither quite so numerous nor so glaring as at first, yet the critic perpetually perceives faults which he had not perceived before. Negligences appear which he had overlooked and even defects show up which had passed as benefits before. He finds much to amend and even to erase in what he had previously admired. When by rigorous reprimands the most acknowledged faults are corrected, his critical discernment, improved by exercise and a greater familiarity with his subject, still detects and will forever detect new imperfections. But he neither throws aside his work nor leaves off his criticism. If it does not make the work more perfect, it will at least make the author more humble. Conscious that if it is not quite so bad as it was, it is still an immeasurable distance from the desired excellence.

Is it not astonishing that we should go on repeating periodically, "Search me, O God, and know my faults," yet neglect to try ourselves? Is there not something more like defiance than devotion to invite the inspection of Omniscience to that heart which we ourselves neglect to inspect? How can any of us as Christians solemnly cry out to God, "Seek the ground of my heart, prove me and examine my thoughts, and see if there be any way of wickedness in me," (Ps. 139:23-24) while we neglect to examine our hearts and are afraid of testing our thoughts, dreading to ask if there "be any way of wickedness" in us, knowing that the inquiry ought to lead to the expulsion of sin?

In our self-inquisition let us fortify our virtue by calling things by their proper names. Self-love is particularly ingenious in inventing disguises of this kind. Let us lay them open, strip them bare, face them and give them as little quarter as if they were the faults of another. Let us not call wounded pride sensitivity. Self-love is made up of soft and sickly sensibilities. Not that sensibility which melts at the sorrows of others, but that which cannot endure the least suffering itself. It is alive in every pore where self is concerned. A touch is a wound. It is careless in inflicting pain, but exquisitely awake in feeling it. It defends itself before it is attacked, revenges affronts before they are offered, and resents as an insult the very suspicion of an imperfection.

In order then to unmask our heart, let us not be content to examine our vices, let us examine our virtues also, "those smaller faults." Let us scrutinize to the bottom those qualities and actions which have more particularly obtained public estimation. Let us inquire if they were genuine in the motivation, singular in the intention, and honest in the prosecution. Let us ask ourselves if in some admired instances our generosity had any trace of vanity, our charity any taint of ostentation. We must question whether when we did such a right action which brought us credit, would we have persisted in doing it if we had foreseen that it would incur censure? Do we never deceive ourselves by mistaking a natural indifference of disposition for Christian moderation? Do we never transform our love of ease into deadness of the world? Do we make our carnal activity into Christian zeal? Do we mistake our obstinacy for firmness, our pride for fortitude, our selfishness for feeling, our love of controversy for the love of God, and our indolence of temper for deadness to human applause? When we have stripped our good qualities bare, when we have made all due deductions for natural temperament, easiness of disposition, self-interest, desire of admiration, of every nonessential attachment, every illegitimate motive, let us fairly add up the account; and we shall be mortified to see how little there will remain. Pride may impose itself upon us even in the guise of repentance. The humble Christian is grieved at his faults; the proud man is angry at them. He is indignant when he discovers he has done wrong, not so much because his sin offends God, but because it has let him see that he is not quite so good as he had tried to make himself believe.

It is more necessary to stimulate us to the humbling of our pride than to the performance of certain good actions. The former is more difficult and it is less pleasant.

That very pride will of itself stimulate to the performance of many things that are laudable. These performances will reproduce pride since they were produced by it, whereas humility has no outward stimulus. Divine grace alone produces it. It is so far from being energized by the love of fame, that it is not humility till it has laid the desire of fame in the dust.

As we have said, if an actual virtue consists in the dominion over the contrary vice, then humility is the conquest over pride, charity over selfishness. It is not only a victory over the natural disposition, but a substitution of the opposite quality. This proves that all virtue is founded in self-denial and self-denial in self-knowledge, and self-knowledge in self-examination. Pride so insinuates itself in all we do and say and think, that our apparent humility often has its origin in pride. That very impatience which we feel at the perception of our faults is produced by the astonishment at finding that we are not perfect. This sense of our sins should make us humble but not desperate. It should teach us to distrust everything in ourselves, and to hope for everything from God. The more we lay open the wounds which sin has made, the more earnestly shall we seek the remedy which Christ has provided.

But instead of seeking for self-knowledge, we are glancing about us for grounds for self-exaltation. We almost resemble the Pharisee who with so much self-complacency delivered the catalogue of his own virtues and other men's sins. Or like the Tartars, who thought they possessed the qualities of those they murdered, the Pharisee fancied that the sins of which he accused the publican would swell the amount of his own good deeds. Like him we take a few items from memory, and a few more from imagination. Instead of pulling down the edifice which pride has raised, we look around on our good works for buttresses to prop it up. We excuse ourselves from the accusation of many faults by alleging that they are common,

and certainly not unique to ourselves. This is one of the
weakest of our deceits. Faults are not less personally ours
because others commit them. The responsibility for sin
can be divided just as matter can. Is there any lessening
of our responsibility for our sin just because others are
guilty of the same?

Self-love is a very diligent motivation, and generally
has two concerns in hand at the same time. It is as busy
in concealing our own defects as in detecting those of
others, especially those of the wise and good. We might
indeed direct its activity in the latter instance to our own
advantage, for if the faults of good men are injurious to
themselves, they might be rendered profitable to us, if
we were careful to convert them to their true use. But
instead of turning them into a means of promoting our
own watchfulness, we employ them mischievously in two
ways. We lessen our respect for pious characters when
we see the infirmities which are blended with their fine
qualities, and we turn their failings into a justification of
our own, which are not like theirs since ours are
overshadowed with virtues. To admire the excellences of
others without imitating them is fruitless admiration. And
to condemn their errors without avoiding them is
unprofitable judgment.

When we are compelled by our conscience to
acknowledge and regret any fault we have recently
committed, this fault so presses upon our recollection that
we seem to forget that we have any other. This single
error fills our mind and we look at it as through a telescope,
which confines sight to that one object exclusively. Other
sins indeed are more effectually shut out because we are
examining this one. Thus, while the object in question
is magnified, the others seem as if they did not exist.

It seems to be established into a kind of system not
to profit by anything outside us, and not to cultivate a
knowledge of anything within us. Though we are

perpetually remarking on the defect of others, when does the remark lead us to study and to root out the same defects in our own hearts? Almost every day we hear of the death of others, but does it induce us to reflect on death as a thing in which we have an individual concern? We consider the death of a friend as a loss, but seldom apply it as a warning. The death of others we lament, and the faults of others we censure, but how seldom do we make use of the one for our own change, or the other for our own preparation for death?

It is the fashion of the times to try experiments in the arts, in agriculture and philosophy. In every science the diligent professor is always afraid there may be some secret which he has not yet attained, some hidden principle which would reward the labor of discovery, something even which the diligent and intelligent person has actually found out, but which has before this eluded *his* pursuit. Shall the Christian stop short in his scrutiny? Shall he not examine and inquire till he lays hold on the very heart and core of the faith?

Why should experimental philosophy be the prevailing study while experimental religion be branded as the badge of enthusiasm, and the jargon of a hollow profession? Shall we never labor to establish the distinction between appearance and reality, between studying religion critically and embracing it practically; between having our conduct creditable and our heart sanctified? Shall we not aspire to do the best things from the highest motives, and elevate our aims by our attainments? Why should we remain in the vestibule when the sanctuary is open? Why should we be content to dwell in the outer courts when we are invited to enter into the holiest by the blood of Jesus?

Natural reason is not likely to furnish arguments sufficiently convincing, nor motives sufficiently powerful to drive us to a close self-inspection. Our corruptions foster this ignorance. To this they owe their undisputed possession of our hearts. No principle short of Christianity is strong enough to impel us to a study so disagreeable as that of a study of our faults. Humility is the prime grace of Christianity, and this grace can never take root and flourish in a heart that lives in ignorance of itself. If we do not know the greatness and extent of our sins, if we do not know the imperfection of our virtues, the failure of our best resolutions, the sickness of our purest purposes, we cannot be humble. If we are not humble, we cannot be Christians.

But we can ask, is there to be no end to this vigilance? Is there no assigned period when this self-denial may become unnecessary? Is there no given point when we may be freed from this annoying self-inspection? Is the matured Christian to be a slave to the same drudgery as the novice? The true answer is—we may cease to watch when our spiritual enemy ceases to assail. We may cease to be on guard when there is no longer any temptation from without. We may cease our self-denial when there is no more corruption within us. We may give the reins to our imagination when we are sure its tendencies will be toward heaven. We may dismiss repentance when sin is abolished. We may indulge selfishness when we can do it without danger to our souls. We may neglect prayer when we no longer need the favor of God. We may cease to praise Him when He ceases to be gracious to us. To discontinue our vigilance at any time short of this will be to defeat all the virtues we have practiced on earth and to put in danger all our hopes of happiness in heaven.

Chapter 13
Self-Love

"The idol Self," says an excellent old divine, "has made more desolation among men than ever was made in those places where idols were served by human sacrifices. It has preyed more fiercely on human lives than Molech (Jer. 32:35) or the Minotaur."[1]

To worship images is a more obvious idolatry, but scarcely more degrading than to set up self in opposition to God. To devote ourselves to this service is as perfect slavery as the service of God is perfect freedom. If we cannot imitate the sacrifice of Christ in His death, we are called to imitate the sacrifice of Himself in His will. Even the Son of God declared, "I came not to do my own will, but the will of Him who sent me." (John 6:38) This was His grand lesson, this was His distinguishing character. Self-will is the ever flowing fountain of all the evil which deforms our hearts, of all the boiling passions which inflame and disorder society; the root of bitterness

---

[1] The Minotaur was a monster of Greek mythology, half man and half bull, who devoured sacrificial victims from time to time.

on which all its corrupt fruits grow. We set up our own
understanding against the wisdom of God, and our own
passions against the will of God. If we could ascertain
the precise period when sensuality ceased to govern the
animal part of our nature, and pride ceased to govern
the intellectual part, that period would form the most
memorable era of the Christian life; from that moment
on we begin a new date of liberty and happiness; from
that stage we set out on a new career of peace, liberty
and virtue.

Self-love is a Proteus[2] of all shapes, shades and complex-
ions. It has the power of expansions and contractions as
best serves the occasion. There is no crevice so small
through which its subtle essence cannot stretch itself to
fill. It is of all degrees of refinement; so coarse and hungry
as to gorge itself with the grossest adulation, so fastidious
as to require a homage as refined as itself; so artful as
to elude the detection of ordinary observers, so specious
as to escape the observation of the very heart in which
it reigns paramount; yet, though so extravagant in its
appetites, it can adopt a moderation which imposes, a
delicacy which veils its deformity, an artificial character
which keeps its real one out of sight.

We are apt to speak of self-love as if it were only a
symptom, whereas it is the disease itself. It is a malignant
disease which has possession of the moral constitution
and leaves nothing uncorrupted by its touch. This
corrupting principle pollutes, by coming into contact with
it, whatever is in itself great and noble. The poet, Alexander
Pope, erroneously called self-love "a little pebble that
stirred the lake, and made it the well-spring of human
progress." His lines are as follows:

---

[2] Proteus was a sea god in Greek mythology who could change his
shape and appearance at will.

Self-love thus push'd to social, to divine,
Gives thee to make thy neighbor's blessing thine.
Self-love but serves the virtuous mind to make
As a small pebble stirs the peaceful lake.

The Apostle James appears to have been of a different opinion from Pope. James speaks as if he suspected that the pebble stirred the lake a little too roughly. He traces this mischievous principle from its birth to the largest extent of its malign influence. The question, "whence come wars and fightings among you?" he answers by another question: "come they not hence, even of your lusts that war in your members?" (Jas. 4:1)

The same pervading spirit which creates hostility between nations, creates animosity among neighbors and discord in families. It is the same principle which, having in the beginning made "Cain the first male child" a murderer in his father's house, has been ever since in perpetual operation. It has been transmitted in one unbroken line of succession through that long chain of crimes of which history is composed, to the present triumphant spoiler of Europe [Napoleon]. In cultivated societies, laws repress the overt act in private individuals by punishment, but the Christian religion is the only thing that has ever been devised to cleanse the spring.

"The heart is deceitful above all things and desperately wicked, who can know it?" (Jer. 17:9) This proposition, this interrogation, we read with complacency, and both the statement and the question being a portion of Scripture, we think it would not be decent to contradict it. We read it, however, with a secret reservation that it is only the heart of all the rest of the world that is meant, and we rarely make the application which the Scripture intended. Each hopes that there is *one* heart that might escape the charge, and he makes the single exception in favor of his own. But if the exception which everyone makes were true, there would not be a deceitful or wicked heart in the world.

As a theory we are ready enough to admire self-knowledge, but when it comes to practice, we are as blindfolded as if our happiness depended on our ignorance. To lay hold on a religious truth, and to maintain our hold, is no easy matter. We like to have an intellectual knowledge of divine things, but to cultivate a spiritual acquaintance with them cannot be easily achieved. We can even force ourselves to believe that which we do not understand more easily than we can bring ourselves to choose that which crosses our will or our passions. One of the first duties of a Christian is to endeavor to conquer this antipathy to the self-denying doctrines against which the human heart so sturdily holds out. The learner takes incredible pains for the acquisition of knowledge. The philosopher cheerfully consumes the midnight oil in his laborious pursuits; he willingly sacrifices food and rest to conquer a difficulty in science. Here the labor is pleasant, the fatigue is welcome, the very difficulty is not without its charms. Why do we react so differently in our religious pursuits? Because in the most laborious human studies, there is no opposition to the will, there is no combat of the affections. If the passions are at all implicated, if self-love is at all concerned, it is rather in the way of gratification than of opposition.

There is such a thing as a mechanical Christianity. There are good imitations of religion, so well executed and so resembling as not only to deceive the spectator but the artist. If properly used, the careful reading of pious books is one of the most beneficial means to preserve us from the influence of self-love.

These very books, however, in the hands of the lazy and self-satisfied, produce an effect directly contrary to that which they were intended to produce, and which they actually do produce on minds properly prepared for them. *They inflate where they were intended to humble.* Some hypochondriacs amuse their melancholy hours by consulting every available medical book, and fancy they can find their own ailment in the ailment of every patient, till they believe they actually feel every pain of which they read, though they read a case diametrically opposite to their own. So the religious soul, weakened by self-love, may be unreasonably elated as the others are discouraged when reading books that describe a religious state far beyond their own. He feels his spiritual pulse by a watch that has no rhythm in common with it, yet he fancies that they go exactly alike. He dwells with delight on symptoms, not one of which belongs to him, and flatters himself with their supposed agreement. He looks in those books for signs of grace, and he observes them with complete self-application; he traces the evidences of being in God's favor, and those evidences he finds in himself.

Self-ignorance appropriates truths faithfully stated but wholly inapplicable. The presumption of the novice arrogates to itself the experience of the advanced Christian. He is persuaded that it is his own case and seizes on the consolations which belong only to the most elevated piety. *Self-knowledge would correct the judgment.* It would teach us to use the pattern held out as an original to copy, instead of leading us to fancy that we are already wrought into the likeness. It would teach us when we read the history of an established Christian, to labor after a conformity to it, instead of mistaking it for the description of our own character.

Human prudence, daily experience, self-love, all teach us to distrust others, but all motives combined do not teach us to distrust ourselves; we confide unreservedly in our own heart, though as a guide it misleads, as a counsellor it betrays. It is both defendant and judge. Self-love blinds the defendant through ignorance; and moves the judge to acquit through partiality.

Though we praise ourselves for our discretion in not confiding too implicitly in others, yet it would be difficult to find any friend, neighbor, or even an enemy who has deceived us so often as we have deceived ourselves. If an acquaintance betray us, we take warning, are on the watch, and are careful not to trust him again. But however frequently the bosom traitor deceive and mislead, no such determined stand is made against his treachery: we lie as open to his next treachery: we lie as open to his next assault as if he had never betrayed us. We do not profit by the remembrance of the past delusion to guard against the future.

Yet if another deceive us, it is only in matters respecting this world, but we deceive ourselves in things of eternal importance. The treachery of others can only affect our fortune or our fame, or at worst, our peace; but the eternal traitor may mislead us to our everlasting destruction. We are too much disposed to suspect others who probably have neither the inclination nor the power to injure us, but we seldom suspect our own heart, though it possesses and uses both. We ought however fairly to distinguish between the simple vanity and the hypocrisy of self-love. Those who content themselves with talking as if the praise of virtue implied the practice, and who expect to be thought good because they commend goodness, only propagate the deceit which has misled them. Hypocrisy, on the other hand, does not even believe herself. She has deeper motives, she has designs to answer, competitions to promote, projects to effect. But mere vanity can subsist on the thin air of the admiration she solicits, without intending to get anything by it. She is gratuitous in her loquacity; for she is ready to display her own merit to those who have nothing to give in return, whose applause brings no profit, and whose censure no disgrace. Self-love feels strengthened by the number of voices in its favor, and is less anxious about the goodness of the work than the loudness of the acclamation. Success is merit in the eyes of both.

But even though we may put more refinement into our self-love, it is self-love still. No subtlety of reasoning, no elegance of taste, though it may disguise the inmost motive, can destroy it. We are still too much in love with flattery even though we may profess to despise that praise which depends on the acclamations of the masses. But if we are over-anxious for the admiration of the better born and the better bred, this by no means proves that we are not vain, it only proves that our vanity has better taste. Our appetite is not coarse enough perhaps to relish that popularity which ordinary ambition covets, but do we never feed in secret on the applause of more distinguishing judges? Is not their having extolled *our* merit a confirmation of their discernment, and the chief ground of our high opinion of *theirs?*

But if any circumstances arise to induce them to change the too-favorable opinion which they had formed of us, though their general character remain as unimpeachable as when we most admired them, do we not begin to judge them unfavorably? Do we not begin to question their claim to that discernment which we ascribed to them, to suspect the soundness of their judgment on which we had commented so loudly? We do well if we do not entertain some doubt of the uprightness of their motive, as we probably question the reality of their friendship. We do not candidly allow for the effect which prejudice, which misinformation, which partiality may produce even on an upright mind. Still less does it enter into our calculation that we may actually have deserved their disapproval, that something in our conduct may have incurred the change in theirs.

It is no low attainment to detect this lurking injustice

in our hearts, to strive against it, to pray against it, and especially to conquer it. We may consider that we have acquired a sound principle of integrity when prejudice no longer blinds our judgment, when resentment does not bias our justice and when we do not make our opinion of others correspond to the opinion they entertain of us. We must have no false estimate which shall incline us to condemnation of others, or to partiality to ourselves. The principle of impartiality must be kept sound or our determinations will not be accurate.

In order to strengthen this principle, we should make it a test of our sincerity to search out and to commend the good qualities of those who do not like us. But this must be done without affectation, and without insincerity. We must practice no false candor. If we are not on our guard, we may be seeking praise for our generosity, while we are only being just. These refinements of self-love are the dangers only of spirits of the higher order, but to such they are dangers.

The ingenuity of self-love is inexhaustible. If people extol us, we feel our good opinion of ourselves confirmed. If they dislike us, we do not think the worse of ourselves, but of them; it is not we who lack merit, but they who lack true insight. We persuade ourselves that they are not so much insensible to our worth as jealous of it. There is no shift, stratagem, or device which we do not employ to make us stand well with ourselves.

We are too apt to calculate unfairly in two ways: by referring to some one signal act of generosity, as if such acts were the common habit of our lives; and by treating our habitual faults, not as common habits, but occasional failures. There is scarcely any fault in another which offends us more than vanity, though perhaps there is none that really injures us so little. We have no patience that another should be as full of self-love as we allow ourselves to be; so full of himself as to have little leisure to pay attention to us. We are particularly quick-sighted to the smallest of his imperfections which interferes with our self-esteem, while we are lenient to his more grave offenses which, by not coming in contact with our vanity, do not shock our self-love.

Is it not strange that though we love ourselves so much better than we love any other person, yet there is hardly one, however little we value him, that we had not rather be alone with, that we had not rather converse with, that we had not rather come to close quarters with, than ourselves? Scarcely one whose private history, whose thoughts, feelings, actions and motives we had not rather pry into than our own? Do we not use every art and contrivance to avoid getting at the truth of our own character? Do we not endeavor to keep ourselves ignorant of what everyone else knows respecting our faults, and do we not account that man our enemy who takes on himself the best office of a friend—that of opening to us our real state and condition?

The little satisfaction people find when they faithfully look within makes them fly more eagerly to the things without. Early practice and long habit might conquer the repugnance to look at home, and the fondness for looking abroad. We might perhaps collect a reasonably just knowledge of our own character if we could ascertain the *real* opinions of others concerning us. But that opinion being, except in a moment of resentment, carefully kept from us by our own precautions, profits us nothing. We do not choose to know their secret sentiments because we do not choose to be cured of our error; because we "love darkness rather than light;" because we conceive that in parting with our vanity, we should part with the only comfort we have, that of being ignorant of our own faults.

Self-knowledge would materially contribute to our

happiness by curing us of that self-sufficiency which is continually exposing us to mortifications. The hourly rubs and vexations which pride undergoes are far more than equivalents for the short intoxications of pleasure which they snatch.

The enemy within is always in a confederacy with the enemy without, whether that enemy be the world or the devil. The domestic foe accommodates itself to their allurements, flatters our weaknesses, throws a veil over our vices, tarnishes our good deeds, guilds our bad ones, hoodwinks our judgment, and works hard to conceal our internal springs of action.

Self-love has the talent of imitating whatever the world admires, even though it should happen to be Christian virtues. Because we regard our reputation, self-love leads us to avoid all vices, not only to escape punishment but disgrace if we committed them. It can even assume the zeal and copy the activity of Christian charity. It attributes to our conduct those proprieties and graces which are manifested in the conduct of those who are actuated by a sounder motive. The difference lies in the ends proposed. The object of the one is to please God, of the other, to win the praises of people.

Self-love, judging the feelings of others by its own, is aware that nothing excites so much odium as its own character would do if nakedly exhibited. We feel, by our own disgust at its exhibition in others, how much disgust we ourselves should excite if we did not clothe it with gentle manners and a polished address. Where therefore we would not condescend "to take the lowest place, to think others better than ourselves, to be courteous and pitiful," on the true Scripture ground, politeness steps in as the accredited substitute of humility, and the counterfeit "paste" is willingly worn by those who will not go to the expense of the real jewel.

There is a certain elegance of mind which will often

restrain a well-bred man from sordid pleasures and gross sensualism. He will be led by his good taste perhaps not only to abhor the excesses of vice, but to admire the theory of virtue. But it is only the excesses of vice which he will abhor. Exquisite gratification, sober luxury, incessant but not unmeasured enjoyment form the principle of his plan of life. If he observes a temperance in his pleasures, it is only because excess would take off the edge, destroy the zest, and abridge the gratification. By resisting gross vice he flatters himself that he is a temperate man and that he has made all the sacrifices which self-denial imposes. Inwardly satisfied, he compares himself with those who have sunk into coarser indulgences, and he enjoys his own superiority in health, credit and unimpaired faculties, and exults in the dignity of his own character.

There is, if the expression may be allowed, a sort of religious self-deceit and affectation of humility which is in reality full of self, which is entirely occupied with self, and which only looks at things as they refer to self. This religious vanity operates in two ways. First, we not only lash out at the imputation of the smallest individual fault, while at the same time we pretend to charge ourselves with more corruption than is attributed to us. On the other hand, while we are lamenting our general lack of all goodness, we fight for every particle that is questioned. The one quality that is in question always happens to be the very one to which we must lay claim, however deficient in others. Thus, while renouncing the pretension to every virtue, "we depreciate ourselves into all." We had rather talk even of our faults than not occupy the foreground of the canvas.

Humility does not consist in telling our faults, but in hearing to be told of them, in hearing them patiently and even thankfully; in correcting ourselves when told, in not hating those who tell us of them. If we were little in our own eyes, and felt our real insignificance, we should avoid false humility as much as mere obvious vanity. But we seldom dwell on our faults except in a general way, rarely on those of which we are really guilty. We do it in the hope of being contradicted, and thus of being confirmed in the secret good opinion we hold of ourselves. It is not enough that we inveigh against ourselves. We must in a manner forget ourselves. This oblivion of self from a pure principle would go further towards our advancement in Christian virtue than the most splendid actions performed on the opposite ground.

That self-knowledge which teaches us humility teaches us compassion also. The sick pity the sick. They sympathize with the disorder of which they feel the symptoms in themselves. Self-knowledge also checks injustice by establishing the equitable principle of showing the kindness we expect to receive. It represses ambition by convincing us how little we are entitled to superiority. It renders adversity profitable by letting us see how much we deserve it. It makes prosperity safe, by directing our hearts to Him who confers it, instead of receiving it as the consequence of our own deserving.

We even carry our self-importance to the foot of the throne of God. When prostrate there we are not required, it is true, to forget ourselves, but we are required to remember HIM. We have indeed much sin to lament, but we have also much mercy to adore. We have much to ask, but we have likewise much to acknowledge. Yet our infinite obligations to God do not fill our hearts half as much as a petty uneasiness of our own, nor HIS infinite perfections as much as our own smallest need! The great, the only effectual antidote to self-love is to get the love of God and of our neighbor firmly rooted in the heart. Yet let us ever bear in mind that dependence on our fellow creatures is as carefully to be avoided as love of them is to be cultivated. There is none but God on whom the principle of love and dependence form but a single duty.

Chapter 14
Our Relations with Non-Christians

As serious Christians our relationships with unbelievers should exhibit a combination of integrity and discretion. We must consider ourselves not only as having our own reputation, but the honor of Christianity in our keeping. While we must, on the one hand, set our face as a flint against anything that may be construed as compromising, denying or concealing any Christian truth in order to curry favor, we must, on the other hand, be very careful never to maintain a Christian point of view with an unchristian disposition. When trying to convince others we must be cautious not to irritate them needlessly. We must distinguish between upholding God's honor and vindicating our own pride, and we must be careful never to stubbornly support the one under the guise of maintaining the other. The resultant dislike of the messenger will be quickly transferred to his God, and the adversary's unfavorable opinion of religion will be magnified by the faults of its champion. At the same time the intemperate champion disqualifies himself from being of any future service to the person who had been offended by his offensive manner.

As serious Christians we feel an honest indignation at hearing those truths treated so lightly on which our everlasting hopes depend. We cannot but feel our hearts rise at the affront offered to our Maker. But instead of calling down fire from heaven on the reviler's head, we should raise a secret supplication to God, which, if it does not change the heart of the opponent, will not only tranquilize our own, but soften it toward our adversary. We cannot easily hate the person for whom we pray.

Those of us who advocate the sacred cause of Christianity should be keenly aware that our being religious will never atone for our being disagreeable. Our orthodoxy will not justify our uncharitableness, nor will our zeal make up for our indiscretion. We must not persuade ourselves that we have been serving God when we have only been indulging our own resentment. A fiery defense may actually prejudice the cause we might perhaps have advanced by a more temperate argument. Keeping a judicious silence when we are being provoked may be painful, but the pain and grief borne in silence will show real forbearance.

Sometimes we hear unwise Christians boasting about the attacks which their own indiscretion has invited. With more vanity than truth they apply the strong and ill-chosen term "persecution" to the sneers and ridicule which some impropriety on their part has occasioned. Now and then it is to be feared the censure may be deserved, and the noble defender of the Christian faith may possibly be only displaying his fallen nature. Even a good man may be blameable in some instances, for which his censurers will naturally have to keep a keen eye. How necessary it is on these occasions to remember that our Lord cautioned us to distinguish for whose sake we are being scorned. Peter also warned us, "If you are reproached for the name of Christ you are blessed. . . . But let none of you suffer as a murderer, or a thief, or a wrongdoer, or a mischief-maker. . . ." (I Pet. 4:14a, 15a)

This close scrutiny by worldly men of those who profess to be Christians is not without very important uses. It serves to promote circumspection in the real Christian, and the detection of those who are insincere, forming a broad and useful line of distinction between these two classes of characters that are frequently but erroneously confused.

The world believes, or at least pretends to believe, that the correct and elegant-minded Christian is oblivious to negative traits such as eccentricity, bad taste, and a propensity to stray from the straight line of prudence, and his adversaries delight to see this. But if the more mature Christians tolerate those infirmities in others, it is not because they do not clearly perceive and entirely condemn them. We bear with them only for the sake of their zeal, sincerity and the general usefulness of these imperfect Christians. Their good qualities are totally overlooked by the censurer, who is ever attempting to exaggerate the failings which Christian charity laments without excusing. Compassion bears with them, believing that impropriety is less harmful than carelessness, bad judgment less harmful than a bad heart, and some little excess of zeal better than gross immorality or total indifference.

We are not ignorant of how much truth itself offends. It is important therefore, not to add to the unavoidable offense by mixing the faults of our own character with the cause we support, because we may be certain that the enemy will take care never to separate them. He will always maintain the fatal association in his own mind. He will never think or speak of the Christian faith without associating it with the real or imputed bad qualities of Christian people he knows or has heard of.

Let not then the friends of truth unnecessarily increase the number of her enemies. Let her not have to sustain

the assaults which her divine character inevitably subjects
her to, with the infirmities and foibles of her unwise or
unworthy champions. But we sometimes justify our rash
behavior under the pretext that our superior spirituality
cannot tolerate the faults of others. The Pharisee
overflowing with wickedness himself, made the exactness
of his own virtue a pretense for looking with horror on
the publican, whom our Savior regarded with compassionate tenderness, while He strongly condemned the
hypocritical attitude of his accuser. "Compassion," says an
admirable French writer, "is that law which Jesus Christ
came down to bring to the world, to repair the divisions
which sin has introduced into it; to be the proof of the
reconciliation of man with God, by bringing him into
obedience to the divine law; to reconcile him to Himself
by subjugating his passions to his reason; and finally, to
reconcile him to all mankind by curing him of the desire
to domineer over them."

But we disqualify ourselves from becoming the
instruments of God in promoting the spiritual good of
anyone if we obstruct the avenue to his heart through
our imprudence. We not only disqualify ourselves from
doing good to all whom we disgust, but should we not
take some responsibility for the failure of all the good
we might have done them if we had not forfeited our
influence by our indiscretion? If we do not assist others
with their spiritual and bodily needs, Christ will consider
it as not having been done to Himself. Our own reputation
is so inseparably connected with that of Christianity that
we should be careful of one for the sake of the other.

The methods of doing good in society are various. We
should sharpen our discernment to discover them and
our zeal to put them in practice. If we cannot open a
man's eyes to the truth of our faith by our arguments,

we may perhaps open them to its beauty by our moderation. Though he may dislike Christianity in itself, he may, admiring the forbearance of the Christian, be at last led to admire the Christian's God. If he has hitherto refused to listen to the written evidences of faith, the temperament of her advocate may be evidence of such an engaging kind that his heart may be opened by the sweetness of the one to the truth of the other. He will at least allow that faith cannot be so bad when its fruits are so agreeable. The conduct of the disciple may in time bring him to the feet of the Master. A new combination may be formed in his mind. He may begin to see what he had supposed as opposites are now being reconciled. He may begin to couple honesty with Christianity.

But if the mild advocate fails to convince, he may attract. Even if he fails to attract, he will at least leave on the mind of the adversary such favorable impressions as may induce him to inquire further. He may be able to engage him on some future occasion with better results, enlarging on the entrance his restraint will have obtained for him.

But even if the temperate pleader should not be so fortunate as to produce any considerable effect on the mind of his antagonist, he is still benefitting of his own soul. He is at least imitating the faith and patience of the saints; he is cultivating that meek and quiet spirit which his blessed Master commanded and commended.

If all bitterness, malice and evil-speaking are expressly forbidden in ordinary cases, surely the prohibition must more particularly apply in the case of religious controversy. Suppose Voltaire and Hume had received their impression of our faith (as one would really suppose they had) from the defenses of Christianity by their able contemporary, Bishop Warburton. They saw this Goliath of learning delivering his ponderous blows, attacking with the same powerful weapons both the enemies of Christianity and also its friends who disagreed with him on points of faith.

He did not meet them as his opponents but pounced on them as his prey, not seeking to defend himself but delighting in unprovoked hostility. When Voltaire and Hume saw Warburton's tactics, would they not exclaim with pleasure, "See how these Christians *hate* one another"? On the other hand, had Warburton's vast powers of mind and knowledge been sanctified by the angelic meekness of Archbishop Leighton, they would have been compelled to acknowledge, if Christianity is false, it is after all so amiable that it deserves to be true.

If we aspired to furnish the most complete triumph to infidels, contentious theology would be our best device. They enjoy the wounds the combatants inflict on each other, not so much from the personal injury which either might sustain as from the conviction that every attack, however it may end, weakens the Christian cause. In all engagements with a foreign foe, they know that Christianity *must* come off triumphantly, therefore all their hopes are founded on attacks within Christianity itself.

If a forbearing temper should be maintained towards unbelievers, how much more towards those who share the same faith. As it is deplorable that there is so much hostility carried on by good men who profess the same faith, so it is a striking proof of the contentiousness of human nature that people can overlook larger problems (slavery, e.g., difficulties that conscience ought not to ignore) and fight over the smaller details, details so insignificant that the world would not even know they existed if the disputants were not so impatient to inform it by their ill-tempered arguments.

While we should never withhold a clear and honest confession of the great tenets of our faith, let us discreetly avoid dwelling on minor distinctions, since they do not affect the essentials either of faith or practice. In this way we may allow others to maintain their opinions while we steadily hold fast our own.

It almost seems that the smaller the point being contested the greater the hostility. We can remember when two great nations were on the point of war over a small parcel of land in another hemisphere. It was so little known that the very name had scarcely reached us, so inconsiderable that its possession would have added nothing to the strength of either. So in theological disputes, more stress is often laid on the most insignificant things.

Is this the catholic spirit which embraces with compassion all children of our common Father without vindicating or approving their faults or opinions, and like its gracious Author, "would not that any should perish"? (II Pet. 3:9)

A preference for remote opinions over those close at hand is by no means confined to Christians. Gibbons, in his *Decline and Fall of the Roman Empire*, was so passionate an admirer of the prophet Mohammed, as to make one wonder if Gibbons' allegiance was to Islam, and so rapturous an eulogist of Julian the Apostate as to suspect the author to be polytheistic. At the same time, Gibbons shows more respect for the stout orthodoxy of the vehement Athanasius than he shows to the "scanty creed" of a contemporary philosopher and theologian whose cold and comfortless doctrines were much more similar to those of Gibbons himself.

It is a delicate point neither to vindicate the truth in so coarse a manner as to excite a prejudice against it nor to make any concessions for the hope of obtaining popularity. "If it be possible, as much as lieth in you, live peaceably with all men" (Rom. 12:18) can no more mean that we should exhibit a false openness which conciliates at the expense of sincerity, than that we should defend the truth with such an intolerant spirit that we injure our cause by our own indiscretion.

As the apostle beautifully advises us, every Christian should adorn our doctrine, not by power, but "by the meekness and gentleness of Christ." (II Cor. 10:1) But we must carefully avoid adopting the ornamental appearance of an amiable temperament as a substitute for true piety. Condescending manners may be one of the numberless modifications of self-love by which a reputation is often obtained but which is not fairly earned. Carefully to examine whether we please others for their edification or in order to gain praise and popularity, is the bounden duty of a Christian.

We should not be angry with the blind for not seeing, nor with the proud for not acknowledging their blindness. Perhaps we ourselves were once as blind and as proud! We, under their circumstances, might have been more perversely wrong than they are, if we had not been treated by our teachers with more patient tenderness than we are disposed to exercise towards them. Tyre and Sidon, we are assured by Jesus Himself, would have repented had they enjoyed the privileges which Chorazin and Bethsaida threw away. Surely we may, for the love of God and for the love of our opponent's soul, do that which well-bred people do through a concern for politeness. Why should a Christian be more ready to offend against the rule of charity than a gentleman against the law of decorum? Candor in judging is like lack of prejudice in acting; both are statutes of the royal law.

Men also feel that they have a right to their own opinions. It is often more difficult to part with this right than with the opinion itself. If our object be the good of our opponent, if it be to promote the cause of truth and not to contend for victory, we shall remember this. We shall consider what value we put upon our own opinion. Why should our opponent's opinion, though a false one, be less dear to him if he believes it true? This consideration will teach us not to expect too much at first. It will teach us the prudence of seeking some general point in which we cannot fail to agree. This will let him see that we do not differ from him for the sake of differing, and our conciliating spirit may bring him to a willingness to listen to arguments on topics where our disagreement is wider.

In disputing, for instance, with those who wholly reject the divine authority of the Scriptures, we gain nothing by quoting them and insisting vehemently on the proof which is to be drawn from them, to support our point in the debate. Their unquestionable truth avails nothing to those who will not allow it. But if we take some common ground on which both parties can stand, and reason from the analogies of natural religion and the recognized course of God's providence, to the ways in which He has declared He will deal with us as revealed in the Bible, our opponent may be struck with the similarity. He then may be more disposed to considerations which may end in the happiest manner. He may finally become less averse to listening to us and accept beliefs which he might otherwise never have seen as having any value.

Where a disputant cannot endure what he sneeringly calls the strictness of evangelical religion, he will have no objection to acknowledging the momentous truths of man's responsibility to his Maker, of the omniscience, omnipresence, majesty and purity of God. Strive then to meet him on these grounds and respectfully ask him if he can sincerely affirm that he is acting upon the truths he already acknowledges. Is he living and acting in all respects as an accountable person ought to live and is he really conscious that he is continually under the eye of a just and holy God? You will find he cannot stand on these grounds. Either he must be contented to receive the truth as revealed in the Gospel, or be convicted of inconsistency or self- deceit or hypocrisy. You will at least make his own ground untenable, if you cannot, indeed, bring him over to yours. But while the opponent is effecting his retreat, do not cut off the means of his return.

Some Christians approve Christianity as knowledge rather than as truth. They like it as it enlarges their view of things, opens to them a wider field of inquiry, a fresh source of discovery and another topic of critical investigation. They consider it as extending the limits of their research rather than as a means of changing their lives. It furnishes their understanding with a fund of riches on which they are eager to draw, not so much for the improvement of the heart as of the intellect. They consider it a thesis on which to raise interesting discussions rather than as promises from which to build a rule of life.

There is something in the presentation of sacred subjects by these persons which according to our conception is not only mistaken but dangerous. We refer to their treatment of faith as a mere science divested of its practical application, taken as a code of philosophical speculation rather than of active belief.

After they have spent half a life upon proofs, which is a mere vestibule to be passed through on the way into the temple of Christianity, we accompany them into *their* edifice and find it composed of materials all too identical with their former taste. Questions of criticism, grammar, history, metaphysics; questions of mathematics and sciences meet us in what St Paul calls the place where "charity out of a pure heart and of a good conscience, and of faith unfeigned, from which" he adds, "some having swerved, have turned aside to vain jangling." (I Tim. 1:5-6)

We do not mean to apply this term "jangling" to all scientific discussions of faith, for we would be the last to deny their use or question their necessity. Our main objection lies in the supremacy given to such topics by our disputants and to the spirit too often manifested in their discussions. It is a preponderance which makes us fear that they consider *these things* as faith itself, as substitutes rather than aids and allies of devotion. At the same time, a cold and philosophical spirit studiously maintained seems to confirm the suspicion that religion with them is not inadvertently, but essentially and solely an exercise of the wits, a field for display of intellectual prowess as if the salvation of souls were a thing of no importance.

These prize fighters in theology remind us of the philosophers of others schools: we feel as if we were reading Newton against Descartes. The practical part of religion in short is forgotten, and lost in its theories; and what is worst of all, a temperament hostile to the spirit of Christianity is employed to defend or illustrate its positions.

This latter effect might be traced further into another allied cause: the habit of treating religion as a field of knowledge capable of demonstration. On a subject supported only by moral evidence, we lament to see questions dogmatically proved instead of being temperately argued. Nay, we could almost smile at the sight of some intricate and barren novelty in religion *demonstrated* to the satisfaction of some ingenious theorist who draws upon a hundred confutations of every position he maintains. The concealed attitudes of the debate are often such as might make angels weep. Such speculators who are more anxious to make proselytes to their opinion than converts to a principle will not be so likely to convince an opponent, as the Christian who is known to act upon his convictions and whose genuine piety will put life and heart into his reasonings. The opponent probably knows already all the ingenious arguments which books supply. Ingenuity therefore will less likely touch them than godly sincerity, which he cannot help but see that the heart of his antagonist is dictating to his lips. There is a simple energy in pure Christian truth which a false motive imitates in vain. The "knowledge which puffs up" will make few real converts when unaccompanied by the "charity which builds up." (I Cor. 8:1)

To remove prejudices is the bounden duty of a Christian, but we must take care not to remove them by conceding our integrity. We must not wound our conscience to save our credibility. If an ill-bred roughness disgusts another, a dishonest concession undoes oneself. We must remove all obstructions to the reception of truth, but truth itself we must not dilute. In clearing away the impediments, we must secure the principle.

If our own reputation is attacked, we must defend it with every lawful means, and we must not sacrifice that valuable possession to any demand but of conscience, to any call but the imperative call of duty. If our good name is put in competition with any other earthly good, we must preserve it, no matter how dear the other good may be. But if the competition lies between our reputation and our conscience, we have no hesitation in making the sacrifice, costly as it is. Sensitive persons feel that their fame is as dear as life itself, but as Christians we know that it is not life to our souls.

For the same reason that we must not be over-anxious to vindicate our fame, we must be careful to preserve it from any unjust allegation. St Paul has set us an admirable example in both respects, and we should never consider him in one point of view without recollecting his conduct in the other. So profound is his humility that he declares himself "less than the least of all saints." (Eph. 3:8) Not content with his comparative depreciation, he proclaims his actual corruptions. "In me, that is, in my flesh, there is no good thing." (Rom. 7:18) Yet this deep self-abasement did not prevent him from asserting his own worth by declaring that he was not behind the very chief of the apostles. Again, "As the truth of Christ is in me, no man shall stop me of this boasting," he says. (II Cor. 11:10) He then enumerates with a manly dignity, tempered with a noble modesty, a multitude of instances of his unparalleled sufferings and his unrivalled zeal.

Where his own personal feelings were in question, how self-abasing! But where the unjust imputation involved the honor of Christ and the credit of the Christian faith, what carefulness it wrought in him, yea, what clearing of himself; yea what indignation, yea, what zeal!

While we rejoice in the promises annexed to the beatitudes, we should be cautious of applying to ourselves promises which do not belong to us, particularly that which is attached to the last beatitude. When our fame is attacked, let us carefully inquire if we are "suffering for righteousness' sake," (Matt. 5:10) or for our own faults. Let us examine whether we may not deserve the censures we have incurred. Even if we are suffering in the cause of God, may we not have brought discredit on that holy cause by our imprudence, our obstinacy, our vanity; by our zeal without knowledge and our earnestness without moderation? Let us inquire whether our revilers have not some foundation for the charge, whether we have not sought our own glory more than that of God, whether we are not more disappointed at missing the praise which we thought our good works were entitled to bring us, than the wound Christianity may have sustained. Let us ask whether, though our views were right and pure on the whole, we neglected to count the cost and expected unmixed approval, uninterrupted success and a full tide of prosperity, totally forgetting the reproaches received and the shame sustained by the Man of Sorrows.

If we can acquit ourselves as to the general purity of our motives, the general integrity of our conduct and the unfeigned sincerity of our efforts, then we may indeed, though with deep humility, take to ourselves the comfort of this divine beatitude. When we find that men only speak evil of us for *His* sake in whose cause we have labored, however that labor may have been mingled with imperfection, we may indeed "rejoice and be exceeding glad." (Matt. 5:12) Submission may be elevated into gratitude and forgiveness into love.

Chapter 15
Christian Watchfulness

Of all the motives to vigilance and self discipline which Christianity presents, there is not one more powerful than the danger of a slackening in zeal and declining devotion. Would that we could affirm that coldness in religion is confined to the irreligious! If it is melancholy to observe an absence of Christianity where no great profession of it was ever made, it is far more grievous to mark its decline where it once appeared not only to exist but to flourish. We feel the same distinct sort of compassion with which we view the financial distresses of those who have been always indigent, and of those who have fallen into want from a state of opulence. Our concern differs not only in degree but in kind.

These changes are a call to awaken watchfulness, humility and self-inspection in those who think that they stand but need to be vigilant lest they fall. There is not any one circumstance which ought more to alarm and quicken the Christian than that of finding oneself growing languid and indifferent after having made a profession and found progress in the Christian walk. Such indifference gives the irreligious person reason to suspect that either there never was any truth in the profession of the person in question, or that there is no truth in religion itself. Critics will be persuaded that religion is weak and soon exhausted, and that a Christian's faith is by no means sufficiently powerful to carry him on his course. Religion's detractor is assured that piety is only an outer garment, put on for show or convenience, and that when it ceases to be wanted for either, it is laid aside. The evil spreads beyond the one indifferent believer, implying that all religious people are equally unsound or equally deluded, although some may be more prudent, or more fortunate or greater hypocrites than others. After one promising believer falls away, the old suspicion recurs and is confirmed, and the defection of others is thought to be inevitable.

The probability is that the one who fell away never was a sound and genuine Christian. His religion was perhaps entered into accidentally, built on some false ground, produced by some ephemeral cause. Alhough it cannot be fairly judged that he intended by his profession and prominent zeal to deceive others, it is probable that he himself was deceived. Perhaps he was too sure of himself; his early profession was probably rather bold and ostentatious. He may have imprudently fixed his stand on ground so high that it would not be easily tenable, and from which a descent would be all too observable. Although at first he thought he never could be too sure of his own strength, he allowed himself to criticize the infirmities of others, especially those whom he had apparently outstripped. Though they had started together, he had left them behind in the race.

Might it not be a safer course at the outset of the Christian life if a modest and self-distrusting humility were to impose a temporary restraint on the bravado of outward profession. A little knowledge of the human heart, a little suspicion of its deceitfulness, would not only moderate the intemperance of an ill-understood zeal, but would save the credit of the Christian faith, which receives a fresh wound from every desertion from her standard.

Some of the most distinguished Christians in this country began their religious career with this graceful humility. They would not allow their change of character and their adoption of new principles and a new course, to be blazoned abroad until the principles they had adopted were established and worked into their character. Their progress proved to be such as might have been inferred from the modesty of their beginnings. They have gone on with a perseverance which difficulties have only strengthened and experience confirmed, and will through divine aid doubtless go on, shining more and more unto the perfect day.

Now let us return to the less-steady convert. Perhaps religion was only, as we have hinted elsewhere, one pursuit among many which he had taken up when other pursuits had failed, and which he now lays down because his faith, not being rooted and grounded, fails also. It is also possible that the temptations coming from the outside might coincide with the inner failure. If vanity is his infirmity, he will recoil from the pointed disapproval of his superiors. If the love of novelty is his besetting weakness, the very uniqueness and strictness of religion, which first was attractive, now is repulsive. The flattering attention which he received, when his life was so different from the manners of the world, now disgusts him. The very opposition which once animated, now cools him. He is discouraged by the reality of the required Christian self-denial, which in anticipation had appeared so delightful. Perhaps his fancy had been fired by some acts of Christian heroism, which he felt an ambition to imitate. The truth is, religion had only taken hold of his imagination, his heart had been left out of the question.

Perhaps religion was originally seen as something only to be believed, but now he finds that it must be lived. Above all the one falling away did not take into consideration the CONSISTENCY which the Christian life demands. Whereas warm affections rendered the practice of some right actions easy at the beginning, not included in the reckoning were the self-denial, the perseverance, and the renouncing of one's own will to which everyone pledges himself who is enlisted under the banner of Christ. The cross which it was easy to venerate, is found hard to bear.

On the other hand, a faltering Christian might have adopted religion when he was in affliction, and he is now happy. It may have been when he was in bad circumstances, and he is now grown affluent. Or it may have been taken on as something he needed to add to his recommendation to some party or project with which he wanted to associate. It may have been something that would enable him to accomplish certain goals he had in view; or something that, with the new acquaintance he wished to cultivate, might obliterate certain blemishes from his former conduct, and whitewash a somewhat sullied reputation.

Now in his more independent situation, it may be that he is surrounded by temptations, softened by blandishments, allured by pleasures which he never expected would arise to weaken his resolutions. These new enchantments make it not so easy to be pious as when he had little to lose and everything to desire, as when the world wore a frowning, and religion an inviting aspect. Or he is perhaps, by the "changes and chances" of life, transferred from a sober and humble society, where to be religious was honorable, to a more fashionable set of associates, where, as the disclosure of his piety would add nothing to his credit, he began to take pains to conceal it till it has fallen into that gradual oblivion which is the natural consequence of its being kept out of sight.

But we proceed to a far more interesting and important character. While the one whom we have been slightly sketching may by his inconstancy do much harm, this person might by his consistency and perseverance achieve indispensable good. Even the sincere and established Christian needs to keep a vigilant eye upon his own heart, especially if his situation in life be easy, and his course smooth and prosperous. If we do not keep our ground, we do not advance in it. Indeed, it will be a sure proof that we have gone back, if we have not advanced.

In a world so beset with snares even sound Christians may experience a slow but certain decline in devotion, a decline scarcely perceptible at first, but more visible in its subsequent stages. Therefore, when we suspect our hearts of any departure from faithfulness, we should compare ourselves with what we were at the supposed height of our devotiom, and not to any other time. The gradual progress of decline is observable only when these two remote states are brought into contrast.

Among other causes of our loss of interest in Christ is the indiscreet forming of some worldly connection, especially that of marriage. In this union the irreligious more frequently draw away the religious to their side, rather than the contrary which is easily understood by those who are at all acquainted with the human heart.

It is also possible for a sincere but incautious Christian to be led by a strong affection to make some little sacrifices of principle for the advancement of a loved one or for the pursual of a cherished cause. It may be observed in passing that those with the most tender hearts are the most susceptible to these disconcerting affections.

We must also take precautions against letting the wealth or position of another believer influence our intent to be honest with them. We become easily deceived because the film over our spiritual eyes grows gradually thicker, and the change is imperceptible to us. So we rationalize our diminished opposition to the faults of a friendly benefactor. We make slight, temporary concessions, tempering measures which we view now as perhaps too severe, when in fact all we have in mind is how that person or cause will benefit us. At the same time we grow cold in the pursuit of the rest of our duties. We begin to lament that in our present situation we can see only small effects of our labors, not perceiving that God may have withdrawn his blessing.

Many Christian parents may be similarly shortsighted with their children. In our plans for their lives we should neither entertain ambitious views, nor consider methods inconsistent with the strictness of our Christian faith. We must "seek first the Kingdom of God and his righteousness," (Matt. 6:33) avoiding the over-solicitious attitude of many who do not profess our faith. We can cheerfully confide in that gracious and cheering promise, that God who is "both their sun and shield, who will give grace and glory, no good thing will He withhold from them that walk uprightly."(Psalm 84:11)

It is one of the trials of faith appended to the sacred office that its ministers, like Father Abraham are liable to go out "not knowing whither they go," (Heb. 11:8) and this not only at their first entrance into their profession but throughout life, an inconvenience to which no other profession is necessarily liable, a trial which is not perhaps fairly estimated.

This remark will naturally raise a laugh among those who at once hold the ministry in contempt, deride its ministers, and think their well-earned pay lavishly and even unnecessarily bestowed. They will probably exclaim in a sarcastic manner, "It is surely a great cause of commiseration to be transferred from a starving assistantship to a position of financial security, or from the lower class of a country parish to the high society of an affluent church."

While there is the positive aspect of the change from a state of uncertainty to a state of independence, from a life of poverty to comfort, or from a marginal to an affluent provision, we cannot discount the feelings and affections of the heart. While money may be that chief good of which ancient philosophy says so much, there are feelings which a man of acute sensibility values more intimately than silver or gold.

Is it absolutely nothing to resign his local comforts, to break up his local attachments, to have new connections to form, and that frequently at an advanced period of life? Connections perhaps less valuable than those he is quitting? Is it nothing for a faithful Minister to be separated from an affectionate people, a people not only whose friendship but whose progress has constituted his happiness here, as it will make his joy and crown of rejoicing hereafter?

Men of delicate minds estimate things by their affections as well as by their circumstances; to a man of a certain cast of character, a change however advantageous may be rather an exile than a promotion. While he gratefully accepts the good, he receives it with an edifying acknowledgment of the imperfection of the best human things. These considerations we confess add the additional feelings of kindness to their persons and of sympathy with their vicissitudes, to our respect and veneration for their holy office.

To themselves, however, the precarious tenure of their situation presents an instructive emblem of the uncertain condition of human life, of the transitory nature of the world itself. Their liableness to a sudden removal gives them the advantage of being more especially reminded of the necessity and duty of keeping in a continual posture of preparation, having "their loins girded, their shoes on their feet, and their staff in their hand." (Ex. 12:11) They have also the same promises which supported the Israelites in the desert. The same assurance which cheered Abraham may still cheer the true servants of God under all difficulties. "Fear not—I am thy shield and thy exceeding great reward." (Gen. 15:1)

But there are perils on the right hand and on the left. It is not among the least that though a pious Clergyman may at first have tasted with trembling caution of the delicious cup of applause, he may gradually grow, as thirst is increased by indulgence, to drink too deeply of the enchanted chalice. The dangers arising from anything that is good are formidable, because unsuspected. And such are the perils of popularity that we will venture to say that the victorious general who had conquered a kingdom, or the sagacious statesman who had preserved it, is almost in less danger of being spoilt by acclamation than the popular preacher; because, although their danger is likely to happen but once, his is perpetual. Theirs is only on a day of triumph, his day of triumph occurs every week; we mean the admiration he excites. Every fresh success ought to be a fresh motive to humiliation; he who feels this danger will vigilantly guard against swallowing too greedily the indiscriminate and often undistinguishing plaudits which either his doctrines or his manner, his talents or his voice may procure for him.

If he be not prudent as well as pious, he may be brought to humour his audience, and his audience to flatter him with a dangerous emulation, till they will scarcely endure truth itself from any other lips. Nay, he may imperceptibly be led not to be always satisfied with the attention and improvement of his hearers, unless the attention be sweetened by flattery and the improvement followed by exclusive attachment.

The spirit of exclusive fondness generates a spirit of controversy. Some of the followers will rather improve in faulty reasoning to support their views. They will be more busied in opposing Paul to Apollos than looking unto "Jesus, the author and finisher of our faith;" (Heb. 12:2) Religious gossip may substitute for religion itself. A party spirit is thus generated, and Christianity may begin to be considered as a thing to be discussed and disputed, to be heard and talked about, rather than as the productive motivation for virtuous conduct.[1]

We owe, indeed, lively gratitude and affectionate attachment to the Minister who has faithfully laboured for our edification; but the author has sometimes noticed a manner adopted by some injudicious adherents, especially of her own sex, which seems rather to erect their favorite into the head of a sect, than to reverence him as the pastor of a flock. This mode of evincing an attachment, amiable in itself, is doubtless as distressing to the delicacy of the Minister as it is unfavorable to religion, to which it is apt to give an air of partisanship.

May we be allowed to remark on the cause of declension in piety in some ministers who formerly exhibited evident marks of that seriousness in their lives which they continue to urge from the pulpit. May it not be partly due to an unhappy notion that the same exactness in his private devotion, the same watchfulness in his daily conduct, is not equally necessary in the advanced progress as in the first stages of a religious course? He does not desist from warning his hearers of the continual necessity of these things, but is he not in some danger of not applying the necessity to himself? May he not begin to rest satisfied with the preaching without the practice? It is not probable indeed that he goes so far as to establish himself as an exempt case, that he slides from indolence into the exemption, as if its avoidance were not so necessary for

---

[1] This polemic tattle is of a totally different character from that species of religious conversation recommended in the preceding chapter.

him as for others.

Even the very sacredness of his profession is not without a snare. He may repeat the holy offices so often that he may be in danger on the one hand of sinking into the notion that it is a mere profession, or on the other, of so resting in it as to make it supersede the necessity of that strict personal religion with which he set out. He may at least be satisfied with the occasional, without the consistent practice. There is a danger—we advert only to its possibility—that his very exactness in the public exercise of his function may lead him to little justifications of his laxity in secret duties. His zealous exposition of the Scriptures to others may satisfy him, though it does not always lead to a practical application of them to himself.

But God, by requiring exemplary diligence in the devotion of his appointed servants, would heap up in their minds a daily sense of their dependence on him. If he does not continually teach by His Spirit those who teach others, they have little reason to expect success, and that Spirit will not be given where it is not sought; or, which is an awful consideration, may be withdrawn where it had been given and not improved as it might.

Should this unhappily ever be the case, it would almost reduce the minister of Christ to a mere engine, a vehicle through which knowledge was barely to pass, like the ancient oracles who had nothing to do with the information but to convey it. Perhaps the public success of the best men had been, under God, principally owing to this; that their faithful ministration in the Temple has been uniformly preceded and followed by petitions in the closet; that the truths implanted in the one have chiefly flourished from having been watered by the tears and nourished by the prayers of the other.

We will hazard but one more observation on this dangerous and delicate subject. If the indefatigable labourer in his great Master's vineyard, has, as must be the case, produced the desired effect, where his warmest hopes had been excited;—if he feels that he has not benefited others as he had earnestly desired, this is precisely the moment to benefit himself, and is perhaps permitted for that very end. Where his usefulness has been obviously great, the true Christian will be humbled by the recollection that he is only an instrument. Where it has been less, the defeat of his hopes offers the best occasion, which he will not fail to use, for improving his humility. Thus he may always be assured that good has been done somewhere, so that in any case his labour will not have been in vain in the Lord.

Chapter 16
True and False Zeal

One of the most important ends of cultivating self-knowledge is to discover what is the real bent of our mind and which are the strongest tendencies of our character; to discover where our disposition requires restraint, and where we may be safely trusted with some liberty of indulgence. Our religious fervor needs the most consummate prudence to restrain its excesses without freezing its energies.

If, on the contrary, timidity is our natural propensity, we shall be in danger of falling into coldness and inactivity with regard to ourselves, and into passive compliance with the request of others or too easy a conformity with their habits. It will therefore be an evident proof of Christian self-government when a man restrains the outward expression of over-ardent zeal where it would be unseasonable or unsafe; while he will practice the same Christian self-denial if he has a fearful and diffident character, to burst the fetters of timidity where duty requires a holy boldness and when he is called upon to lose all lesser fears in the fear of God.

One of the first objects of a Christian is to get his understanding and his conscience thoroughly enlightened; to take an exact survey, not only of the whole comprehensive scheme of Christianity, but of his own nature; to discover, in order to correct, the defects in his judgment; and to ascertain the deficiencies even of his best qualities. Through ignorance in these respects, though he may be following up some good tendency, though he is even persuaded that he is not wrong in his motive or his purpose, he may yet be wrong in the scope, the mode, or in the application, though right in the principle. He must therefore watch over his better qualities with a suspicious eye and guard his very virtues from deviation and excess.

Zeal is an indispensable ingredient in the composition of a great character. Without it no great eminence, secular or religious, has ever been attained. It is essential to the acquisition of excellence in arts and arms, in learning and piety. Without it no man will be able to reach the perfection of his nature, or to animate others to aim at that perfection. Yet it will surely mislead the dedicated Christian if his knowledge of what is right and just does not keep pace with the principle itself.

Zeal, indeed, is not so much a single virtue, as it is the principle which gives life and coloring, grace and goodness, warmth and energy to every other virtue. It is that feeling which exalts the relish of every duty and sheds a luster in the practice of every virtue. It embellishes every image of the mind with its glowing tints and animates every quality of the heart with its invigorating motion. It may be said of zeal that though by itself it never made a great man, yet no man has ever made himself conspicuously great where it has been lacking.

Many things, however, must concur before we can determine whether zeal is really a virtue or a vice. Those who are contending for the one or for the other will be in the situation of the two knights who, meeting on a crossroad, were on the point of fighting about the composition of a cross that was between them. One insisted it was gold; the other maintained it was silver. The duel was prevented by the interference of a passenger who desired them to change their positions. Both crossed over to the opposite side and found that the cross was gold on one side and silver on the other. Each acknowledged his opponent to be right.

It may be disputed whether fire be a good or an evil. The man who feels himself cheered by its kindly warmth is assured that it is a benefit, but he whose house it has just burned down will give another verdict. Not only the cause, therefore, in which zeal is exercised must be good, but the zeal itself must be under proper regulation. If it is not, it will be like the rapidity of the traveller who gets on the wrong road, carrying him so much the farther out of his way, or if he be on the right road, will carry him involuntarily beyond his destination. That degree of zeal is equally misleading which detains us short of our goal, or which pushes us beyond it.

The Apostle suggests a useful precaution by expressly asserting that it is "in a good cause" that we "must be zealously affected." (Gal. 4:18) This implies a further truth, that where the cause is not good the mischief is proportionate with the zeal. But the possibility of misdirected zeal should not totally discourage us from being zealous.

If the injustice, the intolerance and persecution with which a misguided zeal has so often afflicted the Church of Christ be lamented as a deplorable evil, yet the overruling wisdom of Providence, fashioning good out of evil, made those very calamities the instruments of producing that true and lively zeal to which we owe the glorious band of martyrs and confessors, those brightest ornaments of the best periods of the Church. This effect, though a clear vindication of that divine goodness which suffers evil, is no excuse for the one who perpetuates it.

It is curious to observe the contrary operations of true and false zeal, which though apparently only different modifications of the same quality, are, when brought into contact, repugnant and even destructive to each other. There is no attribute of the human mind where the different effects of the same principle have such a total opposition, for is it not obvious that the same principle which actuates the tyrant in dragging the martyr to the stake, can under another direction, enable the martyr to embrace it?

As a striking proof that the necessity for caution is not imaginary, it has been observed that the Holy Scriptures record more instances of bad zeal than of good zeal. This furnishes the most authoritative argument for regulating this impetuous principle, and for governing it by all those restrictions demanded by a feeling so calculated for good and so capable of evil.

It was zeal, but of a blind and furious character, which produced the massacre on the day of St Bartholomew, a day to which the mournful strains of Job have been so well applied: "Let that day perish. Let it not be joined to the days of the year. Let darkness and the shadow of death stain it." (Job 3:3-5) It was zeal most bloody, combined with a perfidy the most detestable, which inflamed the detestable Florentine [Catherine de Medici], when she, under the alluring mask of a public festivity, contrived a general mass of wholesale destruction. The royal and pontifical assassins, not satisfied with the sin, converted it into a triumph. Medals were struck in honor of a deed which has no parallel in the annals of pagan persecution.[1]

---

[1]   Massacre of Saint Bartholemew's Day: the name given to the murder of the Hugenots (French Protestants) in France, which began on St Bartholomew's Day, August 24, 1572. Its authorship is usually attributed to the king's mother, Catherine de'Medici, but its causes were probably

Even glory did not satisfy the pernicious plotters of this direful tragedy. Devotion was called in to be the crown and consummation of their crime. The blackest hypocrisy was made use of to sanctify the foulest murder. The iniquity could not be complete without solemnly thanking God for its success. The Pope and Cardinals proceeded to St. Mark's Church, where they praised the Almighty for so great a blessing conferred on the See of Rome and the Christian world. A solemn jubilee completed the preposterous pretence. This zeal of devotion was much worse than even the zeal of murder, as thanking God for enabling us to commit a sin is worse than the commission itself. A wicked piety is still more disgusting than a wicked act. God is less offended by the sin itself than by the thank-offering of its perpetrators. It looks like a black attempt to involve the Creator in the crime.

For a complete contrast to this pernicious zeal we need not, blessed be God, travel back into remote history, nor abroad into distant realms. This happy land of civil and religious liberty can furnish a countless catalog of instances of a pure, a wise, and a well directed zeal. Not to swell the list, we will only mention that it has in our own age produced the Society for Promoting Christian Knowledge, the British and Foreign Bible Society, and the abolition of the African slave trade. Three as noble and, we trust,

---

more complex. It began with a plot to murder Coligny, whose influence with the king was dreaded by Catherine and others. Although the plot failed it aroused a good deal of suspicion and both sides prepared for bloodshed. Taking advantage of the presence of many Hugenots in Paris (who had come to attend the marriage of Henry of Navarre and the king's sisters Marguerite) Catherine, backed by others, persuaded the king to strike at them. He consented, and the massacre that began in Paris spread to the provinces, lasting until October 3. One authority states that 50,000 were killed, but 25,000 is probably nearer the mark. Pope Gregory XIII ordered a *Te Deum* and had a medal struck depicting an angel with cross and drawn sword slaying Hugenots. (Adapted from *Encyclopedia Americana*).

as lasting monuments as ever national virtue erected in true piety. These are institutions which bear the authentic stamp of Christianity and embrace the best interests of almost the whole of the habitable globe "without partiality and without hypocrisy."

Why we hear so much in praise of zeal from a certain class of religious characters is partly owing to their having taken up a notion that zeal is necessary for the care of other people's salvation, rather than for their own. Indeed the casual prying into a neighbor's house, though much more entertaining, is not nearly as troublesome as the constant inspection of one's own. It is observable that the outcry against zeal among the irreligious is raised on nearly the same ground as the clamor in its favor by these professors of religion. The former suspect that the zeal of the religionists is consumed in censuring *their* impiety, and in eagerness for *their* conversion, instead of being directed to themselves. This supposed anxiety they resent, and they give a practical proof of their resentment by resolving not to profit by it.

Two very erroneous opinions exist respecting zeal. It is commonly supposed to indicate a lack of charity; actually it is a firm friend rather than an enemy. Indeed, charity is such a reliable criterion of its sincerity, that we should be suspect of zeal which is unaccompanied by this fair ally.

Another opinion equally erroneous is prevalent—that where there is much zeal, there is little or no prudence. Now a sound and sober zeal is not such an idiot as to neglect to provide for its own success by taking every precaution which prudence can suggest. True zeal therefore will be as discreet as it is fervent, well knowing that its warmest efforts will be neither effectual, nor lasting, without those provisions which discretion alone can make.

No quality is ever possessed in perfection where its opposite is lacking; zeal is not Christian fervor, but animal heat, if not associated with charity and prudence.

That most valuable faculty of intellectual man, the judgment, the enlightened, impartial, unbiased judgment must be kept in perpetual use, both to ascertain that the cause be good, and to determine the degree of its importance in any given case, so that we may not blindly assign an undue value to an inferior good. Without the discrimination we may be fighting a windmill when we fancy we are attacking a fort! We must prove not only whether the thing contended for be right, but whether it be essential; whether in our eagerness to attain this lesser good we may not be sacrificing or neglecting things of more real consequence; whether the value we assign to it may not be even imaginary.

Above all we should examine if we contend for a cause chiefly because it happens to fall in with our own feelings or our own party, more than for its intrinsic worth. We should also consider whether we do not wish to distinguish ourselves by our tenacity, rather than being committed to the principle itself.

This zeal, hotly exercised over mere circumstantial or ceremonial differences, has unhappily helped in causing irreparable separations and dissensions in the Christian world, even where the champions on both sides were great and good people. Many of the points over which they have argued were not worth insisting upon where the opponents agreed in the grand fundamentals of faith and practice.

But to consider zeal as a general question, as a thing of everyday experience, we can say that he whose religious devotion is most sincere is likely to be the most zealous. But though zeal is an indication, and even an essential part of sincerity, a burning zeal is sometimes seen where the sincerity is somewhat questionable.

For where zeal is generated by ignorance, it is commonly fostered by self-will. That which we have embraced through false judgment we maintain through false honor. Pride is generally called in to nurse the offspring of error. We frequently see those who are perversely zealous for points which can add nothing to the cause of Christian truth, while they are cold and indifferent about the great things which involve the salvation of man.

Though all significant truths and all indispensable duties are made so obvious in the Bible that those "may run who read it," people tend to argue over issues that are unworthy of the heat they excite. Different systems are built on the same texts, so that he who fights for them is not always sure whether he is right or not, and if he wins his point, he can make no moral use of his victory. The correctness of his argument indeed is not his concern. It is enough that he has conquered. The importance of the object never depended on its worth, but on the opinion of his right to maintain that worth.

The Gospel assigns very different degrees of importance to allowed practices and commanded duties. It by no means censures those who were rigorous in their payment of the most inconsiderable tithes; but since this duty was not only competing with, but preferred before the most important duties, even justice, mercy and faith, the flagrant hypocrisy was pointedly censured by *Meekness* itself. (cf. Matt. 23:23)

This opposition of a scrupulous exactness in paying the petty demand on three paltry herbs to the neglect of the three cardinal Christian virtues, exhibits as complete and instructive a specimen as can be imagined of that frivolous and false zeal which, vanishing in trifles, wholly overlooks those grand points on which hangs eternal life.

This passage serves to corroborate a striking fact, that there is scarcely in Scripture any precept enforced which has not some actual example attached to it. The historical parts of the Bible, therefore, are of inestimable value, were it only on this single ground, that the appended truths and principles so abundantly scattered throughout them are in general so happily illustrated by them. They are not dry aphorisms and cold propositions, which stand singly and disconnected, but precepts growing out of the occasion. The recollection of the principles recalls to mind the instructive story which they enrich, while the reminder of the circumstance impresses the lesson upon the heart. Thus the doctrine like a precious gem is at once preserved and embellished by the narrative being made a frame in which to enshrine it.

True zeal will first exercise itself in the earnest desire to obtain greater illumination in our own minds; in fervent prayer that the growing light may operate to the improvement of our conduct; that the influences of divine grace may become more outwardly perceptible by the increasing correctness of our behavior; that every holy affection may be followed by its correspondent act, whether of obedience or of resignation, of doing, or of suffering.

But the effects of a genuine and enlightened zeal will not stop here. It will be visible in our discourse with those to whom we may possibly be of help. The exercise of our zeal, when not done with a bustling kind of interference and offensive forwardness, is proper and useful. Wherever zeal appears, it will be clearly visible, in the same way that a fire will emit both light and heat. We should labor principally to maintain in our own minds the attitudes which our faith has initiated there. The brightest flame will decay if no means are used to keep it alive. Pure zeal will cherish every holy affection, and by increasing every pious disposition will move us to every duty. It will add new force to our hatred of sin, fresh contrition to our repentance, additional vigor to our resolutions, and will impart increased energy to every virtue. It will give life to our devotions, and spirit to all our actions.

When a true zeal has fixed these right affections in our own hearts, the same principle will, as we have already observed, make us earnest to excite them in others. No good man wishes to go to heaven alone, and none ever wished others to go there without earnestly endeavoring to awaken right affections in them. That will be a false zeal which does not begin with the regulation of our own hearts. That will be a narrow zeal which stops where it begins. A true zeal will extend itself through the whole sphere of its possessor's influence. Christian zeal like Christian charity will begin at home, but neither the one nor the other must end there.

But that we must not confine our zeal to mere conversation is not only implied but expressed in Scripture. The apostle does not exhort us to be zealous only of good *words* but or good *works*. True zeal ever produces true benevolence. It would extend the blessings which we ourselves enjoy to the whole human race. It will consequently stir us up to exert all our influence to the extension of religion, to the advancement of every well conceived and well conducted plan, calculated to enlarge the limits of human happiness, and more especially to promote the eternal interests of humankind.

But if we do not first strenuously labor for our own illumination, how shall we presume to enlighten others? It is a dangerous presumption to busy ourselves in improving others before we have diligently sought our own improvement. Yet it is a vanity not uncommon that the first feelings, be they true or false, which resemble devotion, the first faint ray of knowledge which has imperfectly dawned, excites in certain raw minds an eager impatience to communicate to others what they themselves have not yet attained. Hence the novel swarms of uninstructed instructors, of teachers who have had no time to learn. The act previous to the imparting knowledge should seem to be that of acquiring it. Nothing would so effectually check an irregular zeal for a temperate zeal, as the personal discipline, the self-acquaintance which we have so repeatedly recommended.

True Christian zeal will always be known by its distinguishing and inseparable properties. It will be warm indeed, not from temperament but principle. It will be humble, or it will not be *Christian* zeal. It will restrain its impetuosity that it may the more effectually promote its object. It will be temperate, softening what is strong in the act by gentleness in the manner. It will be tolerating, willing to grant what it would itself desire. It will be forbearing, in the hope that the offence it seeks to correct may be an occasional lapse rather than a habit of the mind. It will be candid, making a tender allowance for those imperfections which beings, fallible themselves, ought to expect from human infirmity. It will be a friendly admonishment, instead of irritating by the adoption of violence, instead of mortifying by the assumption of superiority.

He, who in private society allows himself in violent anger or unhallowed bitterness or acrimonious railing to reprehend the faults of another, might, did his power keep pace with his inclination, have recourse to other weapons. He would probably banish and burn, confiscate and imprison, and think then, as he thinks now, that he is doing God service.

If there be any quality which demands clear sight, a tight rein and a strict watchfulness, zeal is that quality. The heart where zeal is lacking has no true life, where it is not guarded, no security. The prudence with which zeal is exercised is the surest evidence of its integrity; for if intemperate, it raises enemies not only to ourselves but to God. It augments the natural enmity to religion instead of increasing her friends.

But if tempered by charity, if blended with benevolence, if sweetened by kindness, if shown to be honest by its influence on your own conduct, and gentle by its effect on your manners, zeal may lead your irreligious acquaintance to inquire more closely to what distinguishes them from you. You will already by this mildness have won their affections. Your next step may be to gain over their judgment. They may be led to examine what solid grounds of difference exist between us and them, what substantial reason you have for not going their way, and what sound argument they can offer for not going yours.

But it may possibly be asked, after all, where do we perceive any symptoms of this inflammatory distemper? Should not the prevalence, or at least the existence of a disease be ascertained before applying the remedy? That an illness exists is sufficiently obvious, though it must be confessed that among the higher classes it has not hitherto spread very widely. Its progress is not likely to be very alarming, nor its effects very malignant. It is to be lamented that in every class indeed, coldness and indifference, carelessness and neglect, are the reigning epidemics. These are diseases far more difficult to cure, diseases as dangerous to the patient as they are distressing to the physician, who generally finds it more difficult to raise a sluggish habit than to lower an occasional heat. The imprudently zealous man, if he be sincere, may by a discreet regimen, be brought to a state of complete sanity; but to rouse from a state of morbid indifference, to brace from a total relaxation of the system, must be the immediate work of the Great Physician of souls; of Him who can effect even this, by His spirit accompanying this powerful word: "Awake, thou that sleepest, and arise from the dead, and Christ shall give thee light." (Eph. 5:14)

Chapter 17
The Peril of Neglecting Eternal Things

Insensibility to eternal things in beings who are standing on the brink of eternity is a madness which would be considered a wonder if it were not so common. Suppose we had the prospect of inheriting a great estate and a splendid mansion which we knew would be ours in a few days, and in the meantime we rented a paltry cottage in bad repair, ready to fall, and from which we knew we must at all events soon be turned out. Would it be wisdom or common sense to overlook totally our near and noble inheritance and to be so fondly attached to our falling tenement that we spent a great part of our time and thoughts in supporting its ruins by props, and concealing its decay by decorations? To be so absorbed in the little sordid pleasures of this frail abode so as not even to cultivate a taste for the delights of the mansion where such treasures are laid up for us—this is an excess of folly which must be seen to be believed.

It is a striking fact that the recognized uncertainty of

life drives worldly people to make sure of everything except their eternal concerns. It leads them to be up-to-date in their accounts and exact in their transactions. They are afraid of risking even a little property on so precarious a thing as life, without insuring their inheritance. There are some who even speculate on the uncertainty of life as a trade. It is strange that this accurate calculation of the duration of life should not involve a serious attention to its end! Strange, too, that in the prudent care not to risk a fraction of property, equal care should not be taken not to risk eternal salvation!

We are not speaking here of grossly wicked characters. We are not supposing that their wealth has been obtained by injustice or increased by oppression. We are only describing a soul drawn aside from God by the alluring baits of the world. The shining bangles are obtained, but the race is lost!

To worldly people of a more serious nature, business may be as formidable an enemy of the soul as pleasure is to those of a lighter character. Business has so sober an air that it looks like virtue, and virtuous it certainly is when carried on in a proper spirit with due moderation in the fear of God. To have a lawful employment and to pursue it with diligence is not only right and honorable in itself, but is one of the best safeguards against temptation.

We can point out the diligence that business demands, the self-denying practices it imposes, the patience, regularity and industry indispensable to its success. These are habits of virtue that are a daily discipline to a moral person in business. The world, as a matter of fact, could not survive without business. But attention paid to these realities often detracts us from interests in the eternal world, when we can neglect to lay up a treasure in heaven in order to lay up the treasure of earth—a supply which we perhaps do not need and do not intend to use. In this case we are a bad judge of the relative value of things.

Business has an honorable aspect in that it is opposed to idleness, the most hopeless offspring of the whole progeny of sin. Persons in business, comparing themselves with those who squander their living, feel a fair and natural consciousness of their own value and of the superiority of their own pursuits. But it is by making comparisons with others that we deceive ourselves. Business, whether professional, commercial or political, endangers the mind which looks down on the pursuit of pleasure as beneath a thinking being. But if business absorbs the heart's affections, if it swallows up time to the neglect of eternity, if it generates a worldly spirit or encourages covetousness and engages the mind in ambitious pursuits, it may be as dangerous as its more frivolous rival. The grand evil of both lies in the alienation of the heart from God. Actually, in one respect, the danger is greater to the one who is best employed. Those who pursue pleasure, however thoughtless, can never make themselves believe they are doing right. But those plunged in the work of serious business cannot easily persuade themselves that they are doing wrong.

Compensation and trade are the devices which worldly religion incessantly keeps in play. It is a life of barter— so much indulgence for so many good works. The implied accusation is that "we have a rigorous Master," and that therefore it is only fair to pay ourselves for the severity of His demands, just as an overworked servant steals a holiday. They set bounds to God's right to command, lest it should encroach on their privilege to do as they please.

We have mentioned elsewhere that if we invite people to embrace the Christian faith on the grounds that they will obtain present pleasure, they will desert it as soon as they find themselves disappointed. People are too ready to clamor for the pleasures of devotion before they have entitled themselves to them. We would be angry at those employees who asked to receive their wages before they would begin to work. This is not meant to establish the merit of works, but rather the necessity of seeking that transforming and purifying change which marks the real Christian. It is a matter of the heart and a genuine change in one's attitude.

But if we consider this world on true scriptural grounds as a place of testing, and see religion as a school for happiness, the consummation of which is only to be enjoyed in heaven, then the Christian hope will support us and the Christian faith will strengthen us. We can serve diligently, wait patiently, love cordially, obey faithfully and be steadfast under all trials. We can be sustained by the cheering promise held out to those "who endure to the end."

There are some who seem to have a graduated scale of vices. They keep clear of the lowest degrees on this scale, but they are not diligent in avoiding the "highest" vices on their scale. They forget that the same motive which operates in the greater operates on the lesser as well. A life of incessant gratification does not alarm the conscience, but it is surely unfavorable to faith, destructive of its motivations, and opposed to its spirit, as are the more obvious vices.

These are the habits that relax the mind and remove resolve from the heart, thereby fostering indifference to our spiritual state and insensibility to the things of eternity. A life of pleasure, if it leads into a life of actual sin, disqualifies us for holiness, happiness and heaven. It not only alienates the heart from God, but it lays it open to every temptation that natural temperament may invite, or incidental circumstances allure. The worst passions lie dormant in hearts that are given up to selfish indulgences, always ready to start into action as any occasion invites them.

Sensual pleasure and irreligion play into each other's hands: each can cause the other. The slackness of the inward motivation confirms the carelessness of the conduct, while the negligent conduct protects itself under the supposed security of unbelief. The instance of the rich man in the parable of Lazarus strikingly illustrates this truth.

It is as essential that we inquire whether these unfeeling attitudes and selfish habits offend society and discredit us with the world, as it is important that we realize that they feed our corruptions and put us in a position unfavorable to all interior improvement. Let us ask whether they offend God and endanger the soul, whether the gratification of self is the life which the Redeemer taught or lived. Let us ask whether sensuality is a suitable preparation for that state where God Himself, who is Spirit, will constitute all the happiness of spiritual beings.

But these are not the only dangers. The intellectual vices, the spiritual offenses may destroy the soul without much injury to one's reputation. Unlike sensuality, these do not have their seasons of change and repose. Here the motive is in continual operation. Envy has no interruption. Ambition never cools. Pride never sleeps. The inclination to these at least is always awake. An intemperate person is sometimes sober, but a proud person is never humble. Where vanity reigns, it reigns always. These interior sins are more difficult to eradicate. They are harder to detect, harder to come at, and, as the citadel sometimes holds out after the outer defenses of a castle are breached, these sins of the heart are the last conquered in the moral warfare.

Here lies the distinction between the worldly and the religious person. It is frightening enough for the Christian that we feel any propensity to vice. Against these inclinations we must watch, strive and pray. Although we are thankful for the victory when we have resisted the temptation, we feel no elation of heart while conscious of our inward dispositions. Nothing but divine grace enables us to keep them from breaking out into a flame. We feel the only way to obtain the pardon of sin is to stop sinning, that although repentance itself is not a savior, there still can be no salvation where there is no repentance. Above all, we know that the promise of remission of sin by the death of Christ is the only solid ground of comfort. However correct our present life may be, the weight of past offenses would hang so heavy on our conscience that without the atoning blood of our Redeemer, despair of pardon for the past would leave us hopeless. We would continue to sin in the same way that a bankrupt person may continue to be extravagant because no present frugality could redeem their former debts.

It is sometimes pleaded that the work that busy and important people have leaves them no time for their religious duties. These apologies are never offered for the poor man, although to him every day brings the inevitable return of his many hours of work without intermission or moderation.

But surely the more important and responsible the position a person holds, the more demanding is the call for faith, not only in the way of example, but even in the way of success. If it is indeed granted that there is such a thing as divine interventions, if it is allowed that God has a blessing to bestow, then the ordinary man who has only himself to govern requires aid, but how urgent is *the person's* necessity who has to govern millions? What an awful idea that the weight of a nation might rest on the head of one whose heart does not look up for higher support!

The politician, the warrior and the orator find it peculiarly hard to renounce in themselves that wisdom and strength to which they believe the rest of the world is looking up. The person of station or of genius, when invited to the self-denying duties of Christianity often draws back, like the one who went away sorrowing because he had great possessions.

To know that they must come to an end stamps vanity on all the glories of this life. To know that they must come to an end soon stamps *folly,* not only on the one who sacrifices his conscience for their acquisition, but also on the person who, though upright in the discharge of his duties, discharges them without any reference to God. If the conqueror or the orator would reflect when the laurel crown is placed on his brow, how soon it will be followed by the cypress wreath,[1] the delirium of ambition would be cooled and the intoxication of prosperity removed.

There is a general kind of belief in Christianity prevalent in the world which, by soothing the conscience, prevents self-inquiry. That the holy Scriptures contain the will of God they do not question. That they contain the best system of morals, they frequently assert. But they do not feel the necessity of acquiring a correct notion of the teachings those Scriptures contain. The depravity of man, the atonement made by Christ, the work of the Holy Spirit— these they consider as the theoretical part of religion which they can easily neglect. By a kind of self-flattery, they satisfy themselves with the idea that they are acceptable to their Maker, a state they mistakenly believe they can attain without humility, faith and the rebirth of life.

People absorbed in a multitude of secular concerns, decent but unawakened, listen with a kind of respectful insensibility to the overtures of spiritual conviction. They consider the Church as venerable because of her antiquity

---

[1] A bow of black, heavy satin or other material hung on the doorway of a home at the time of death.

and important because of her connection to the state. No
one is more alive to her political, nor more dead to her
spiritual importance. They are anxious for her existence,
but indifferent to her doctrines. These they consider as
a general matter in which they have no personal concern.
They consider religious observances as something
attractive but unreal, a serious custom made respectable
by long and public usage. They admit that the poor who
have little to enjoy and the idle who have little to do,
cannot do better than to give over to God that time which
cannot be turned to more profitable account. Religion,
they think, may properly make use of leisure and occupy
old age. Yet when it comes to themselves, they are at a
loss to determine the precise period when the leisure is
sufficient or the age is enough advanced. Goals recede
as the destined season approaches. They continue to
intend moving, but they continue to stand still.

Compare their drowsy sabbaths with the animation of
the days of business and you would not think they were
the same individual. The one is to be gotten over, the
others are enjoyed. They go from the dull decencies, the
shadowy forms (as they perceive them) of public worship,
to the solid realities of their worldly concerns. These they
consider as their bounden, and exclusive duties. The others
indeed may not be wrong, but these, they are sure, are
right. The world is their element. Here they are
substantially engaged. Here their whole mind is alive, their
understanding wide awake, all their energies in full play.
Here they have an object worthy of their widest expansions,
and here their desires and affections are absorbed. The
faint impression of the Sunday sermon fades away to be
as faintly revived on the following Sunday, again to fade
in the succeeding week. To the sermon they bring a formal
ceremonious attendance. To the world they bring all their
heart, soul, mind and strength. To the one they resort
in conformity to law and custom. To induce them to resort

to the other, they need no law, no sanction, no invitation. Their will is enough. Their passions are volunteers. The invisible things of heaven are clouded in shadow. The world is lord of the present. Riches, honors, power fill their mind with brilliant images. They are certain, tangible, and they assume form and bulk. In these, therefore, they cannot be mistaken. The eagerness of competition and the struggle for superiority fill their mind with an emotion, their soul with an agitation and their affections with an interest which, though very unlike happiness, they deceive themselves into thinking that it is the road to it. This artificial pleasure, this tumultuous feeling, does at least produce that one negative satisfaction of which worldly people are in search—it keeps them from themselves.

Even in circumstances where there is no success, the mere occupation, the crowd of objectives, the succession of engagements and the very tumult and hurry have their gratifications. The bustle gives false peace by leaving no leisure for reflection. They put their consciences to sleep by asserting they have good intentions. They comfort themselves with the believable pretense that they lack time and the vague resolution of giving up to God the dregs of life, while feeling the world deserves the better part of it. Thus commuting with their Maker, life wears away, its end drawing ever nearer, and that delayed promise to give God the last part is not fulfilled. The assigned hour of retreat either never arrives, or if it does arrive, sloth and sensuality are resorted to as a fair reward for a life of labor and anxiety. They die in the shackles of the world.

If we do not earnestly desire to be delivered from the dominion of these worldly tendencies, it is because we do not believe in the condemnation attached to their indulgence. We may indeed believe it as we believe any other general proposition or inconsequential fact, but we do not believe it as a danger which has any reference to *us*. We disclose this practical unbelief in the most unequivocal way by thinking so much more about the most frivolous concern in which we are sure we have an interest, than about this most important of all concerns.

When we are indifferent to eternal things, we add to our peril. If shutting our eyes to a danger would prevent it, to shut them would not only be a happiness but a duty. But to trade eternal safety for momentary ease is a wretched compromise. The reason why we do not value eternal things is because we do not think of them. The mind is so full of what is present that it has no room to admit a thought of what is to come. We are guilty of not giving the same attention to an eternal soul which prudent souls give to a common business transaction. We complain that life is short, and yet throw away the best part of it, only giving over to religion that portion which is good for nothing else. Life would be long enough if we assigned its best period to the best purpose.

Do not say that the requirements of religion are severe. Ask rather if they are necessary. If a thing must absolutely be done and if eternal misery will be incurred by not doing it, it is fruitless to enquire whether it be hard or easy. Inquire only whether it is indispensable, whether it is commanded. The duty on which our eternal state depends is not a thing to be debated, but done. The duty which is too imperative to be evaded is not to be argued about, but performed. To continue quietly in sin because you do not intend to sin is to live on an expected inheritance which will probably never be yours.

It is folly to say that religion drives people to despair when it only teaches them by a healthy fear to avoid destruction. The fear of God differs from all other fear, for it is accompanied with trust, confidence and love. "Blessed is the one who feareth always," is no paradox to one who entertains this holy fear. It sets us above the fear of ordinary troubles. It fills our heart. We are not distraught by those inferior apprehensions which unsettle the soul and unhinge the peace of worldly people. Our mind is occupied with one grand concern and is therefore less liable to be shaken than little minds which are filled with little things. Can that principle lead to despair which proclaims the mercy of God in Jesus Christ to be greater than all the sins in the world?

If *despair* prevents your returning to God, do not add to your list of offenses that of doubting the forgiveness which He sincerely offers. You have already wronged God in His holiness. Do not wrong Him in His mercy. You may offend Him more by despairing of His pardon than by all the sins which have made that pardon necessary. Repentance, if one may venture the bold remark, almost disarms God of the power to punish. Here are His style and title as proclaimed by Himself: "The Lord, the Lord God, merciful and gracious, long-suffering and abundant in goodness and truth, keeping mercy for thousands, forgiving iniquity, transgression and sin, and who will by no means clear the guilty;" (Ex. 34:6-7a) that is, those who by unrepented guilt exclude themselves from the offered mercy.

If unfaithfulness or indifference, which is practical unfaithfulness, keeps you back, then as reasonable beings, ask yourselves a few short questions: For what purpose was I sent into the world? Is my soul immortal? Am I really placed here in a state of trial, or is this span my all? Is there an eternal state? If there is, will the use I make of this life decide my condition in that state? I know there is death, but is there a judgment?

Do not rest until you have cleared up, not your own proofs for heaven (it will be some time before you arrive at that stage) but whether there *is* any heaven. Is not Christianity important enough for you diligently to explore? Is not eternal life too valuable to be entirely overlooked, and eternal destruction, if a reality, worth avoiding? If you make these interrogations sincerely, you will make them practically. They will lead you to examine your own personal interest in these things. Evils which are ruining us for lack of attention lessen from the moment our attention to them begins. True or false, the question is worth settling. Do not waver then between doubt and certainty. If the evidence is inadmissible, reject it. But if you can once ascertain these cardinal points, then throw away your time if you *can, and trifle with eternity if you dare!*

It is one of the striking characteristics of the Almighty that "He is strong and patient." It is a standing evidence of His patience that "He is provoked every day." How beautifully do these characteristics complement each other. If He were not strong, His patience would lack its distinguishing perfection. If He were not patient, His strength would instantly crush those who provoke Him every day.

Oh you, who have a long space given you for repentance, confess that the forbearance of God, when seen as coupled with His strength, is His most astonishing attribute. Think of those whom you knew who have since passed away— companions of your early life, your associates in actual vice, or your confederates in guilty pleasures. They are the sharers of your thoughtless meetings, your jovial revelry, your worldly schemes, your ambitious projects. Think how many of those companions have been cut off, perhaps without warning, possibly without repentance. *They* have been presented to their Judge. Their *doom,* whatever it is, is now fixed. Yours is mercifully suspended. Adore the mercy; embrace the suspension.

Only suppose if they could be permitted to come back to this world, if they were allowed another period of trial, how they would spend their restored life! How earnest would be their penitence, how intense their devotion, how profound their humility, how holy their actions! Think then that you still have in your power that for which they would give millions of worlds. "Hell," says one writer, "is truth seen too late."

In almost every mind there sometimes float indefinite and general purposes of repentance. The operation of these purposes is often repelled by a real, though denied, skepticism. Because the sentence is not executed speedily, they suspect it has never been pronounced. They, therefore, think they may safely continue to defer their intended, but unshaped, purpose. Though they sometimes visit the sickbeds of others and see how much disease disqualifies one from performing all duties, yet it is to this period of incapacity that they continue to defer this vital need to repent.

What an image of the divine condescension does it convey that "the goodness of God leadeth to repentance"! (Rom. 2:4) It does not barely invite, but it conducts. Every warning is more or less an invitation. Every visitation is a lighter stroke to avert a heavier blow. This was the way in which the heathen world understood signs and wonders, and on this interpretation of them they acted. Any alarming warning, whether rational or superstitious, drove them to their temples, their sacrifices. Does our clearer light always carry us farther? Does it, in these instances, always carry us as far as natural conscience carried them?

The final period of the worldly person at length arrives, but they will not believe their danger. Even if they fearfully glance around to every surrounding face, looking for an intimation of it, every face, it is too probable, is in league to deceive them. What a noble opportunity is now offered to the Christian physician to show a kindness far superior to any they have ever shown, just as the concerns of the soul are superior to those of the body! Let them not fear *prudently* to reveal a truth for which the patient may bless them in eternity! Is it sometimes to be feared that in the hope of prolonging for a little while the existence of the perishing body, they rob the never-dying soul of its last chance of pardon? Does not the concern for the immortal part united with their care of the afflicted body bring the Christian physician to a nearer imitation of that divine Physician who never healed the one without manifesting a tender concern for the other?

But the deceit is short and fruitless. The amazed spirit is about to dislodge. Who shall speak of its terror and dismay? Then the person cries out in the bitterness of their soul, "What ability have I, now that I am dying, to acquire a good heart, to unlearn false beliefs, to renounce bad practices and establish right habits, to begin to love God and hate sin?" How is the stupendous concern of salvation to be worked out by a mind incompetent to do it in the most favorable conditions?

The infinite importance of what a person has to do, the goading conviction that it must be done, and the impossibility of beginning a repentance which should have been completed—all these complicated concerns together add to the sufferings of a body which stands in little need of these additional burdens.

It would be well if we were now and then to call to our minds, while in sound health, the solemn certainties of a dying bed. It would be well if we accustomed ourselves to see things now as we shall wish we had seen them. Surely the most sluggish insensibility can be roused by seeing for itself the rapid approach of death, the nearness of our unalterable doom and our instant transition to that state of unutterable blessing or unimaginable woe to which death will in a moment consign us. Such a mental image would assist us in dissipating all other illusions. It would help us realize what is invisible, and to bring near what we think of as remote. It would disenchant us from the world, tear off its painted mask, shrink its pleasures into their proper dimensions, its concerns into their real value, and its promises into nothingness.

Terrible as the evil is, if it must be met, do not hesitate to present it to your imagination. Do this, not to lacerate your feelings, but to arm your resolution, not to arouse more distress, but to strengthen your faith. If it terrifies you at first, draw a little nearer more gradually, and familiarity will lessen the terror. If you cannot face the image, how will you encounter the reality?

Let us then picture for ourselves the moment when all we cling to shall elude our grasp, when every earthly good shall be to us as if it had never been, when our eyes open on the spiritual world. Then there shall be no relief for the fainting body, no refuge for the parting soul except that single refuge to which perhaps we have never thought of resorting—the everlasting mercies of God in Christ Jesus.

Reader! whoever you are who have neglected to remember that to die is the end for which you were born, know that you have a personal interest in this scene. Do not turn away from it in disdain, however feebly it may have been represented. You may escape any other evil of life, but its end you cannot escape. Do not defer then life's weightiest concern to its weakest period. Do not begin the preparation when you should be completing the work. Do not delay the business which demands your best faculties to the period of their greatest weakness and near extinction. Do not leave the work which requires an age to do, to be done in a moment, a moment which may not be granted. The alternative is tremendous. The difference is that of being saved or lost. It is no light thing to perish.

Chapter 18
When Good People Suffer

Affliction is the school in which great virtues are acquired and in which great characters are formed. It is like a spiritual gymnasium in which the disciples of Christ are trained in robust exercise, hardy exertion and severe conflict.

We do not hear of military heroes in peacetime, nor of the most distinguished saints in the quiet and unmolested periods of church history. The courage in the warrior and the devotion in the saint continue to survive, ready to be brought into action when perils beset the country or trials assail the Church, but it must be admitted that in long periods of inaction both are susceptible to decay.

The Christian in our comparatively tranquil day is happily exempt from the trials and terrors which the annals of persecution record. *[The author here refers to the situation in England in the early 19th century. Ed.]* Thanks to the establishment of the church, and thanks to the stability of our laws and to the mild and tolerating spirit of both, one is far from being liable to pains and penalties for his attachment to his religion.

The Christian is still not exempt from his individual trials. We can include those cruel mockings which Paul appropriately ranked in the same list with bonds, imprisonments, exiles and martyrdom itself. We can also add those misrepresentations and attacks to which the zealous Christian is particularly liable. The truly good person is not only called to struggle with trials of large dimensions, but with the daily demands and difficulties of this earthly life.

The pampered Christian, thus continually gravitating to the earth, would have his heart solely bent toward the trials of daily life, unmindful of the crown *God* gives to His true servants when this mortal life is over.

It is an unspeakable blessing that no events are left to the choice of beings who in their blindness would constantly choose wrongly. Were circumstances at our own disposal, we should choose for ourselves nothing but ease and success, nothing but riches and fame, nothing but perpetual youth, health and unmitigated happiness.

We are placed on earth temporarily, and our situation in eternity depends on the use we make of this present time. Therefore nothing would be more dangerous than such a power to choose for ourselves.

If a surgeon were to put into the hand of a wounded patient the probe or the scalpel, how tenderly would he treat himself! How skin-deep would be the examination, how slight the incision! The patient would escape the pain, but the wound might prove fatal. The surgeon therefore wisely uses his instruments himself. He goes deep perhaps, but not deeper than the case demands. The pain may be acute, but the life is preserved.

Thus He in whose hand we are, is too good and loves us too well to trust us with our own surgery. He knows that we will not contradict our own inclinations, that we will not impose on ourselves any voluntary pain, however necessary the infliction, however healthful the effect. God graciously does this for us Himself because otherwise He knows it would never be done.

A Christian is liable to the same sorrows and sufferings as others. Nowhere do we have a promise of immunity from the troubles of life, but we do have a merciful promise of support when we go through them. Therefore we consider them from another view. We bear them with another spirit, utilize them to other purposes than those whose view is limited to this world. Whatever may be the instruments of our suffering, whether sickness, losses, vilification, persecutions, we know that they all proceed from God. All methods are HIS instruments. All secondary causes operate by HIS directing hand.

We said that a Christian is liable to the same sufferings as other men. Might we not repeat what we have said before, that our very Christian profession is often the cause of our sufferings? They are the badge of our discipleship, the evidences of our Father's love. They are at once the marks of God's favor and the preparations for our own future happiness.

What were the arguments held out through the whole New Testament to encourage the world to embrace the faith it taught? What was the condition of St Paul's introduction to Christianity? It was not, "I will crown him with honor and prosperity, with dignity and pleasure," but "I will show him how great things he must suffer for my name's sake." (Acts 9:16)

What were the chief virtues which Christ taught? What were the graces He most recommended by His example? Were they not self-denial, mortification, patience, long-suffering, renouncing ease and pleasure? These are the marks which have always distinguished Christianity from all the other religions of the world, and therefore prove its divine origin. Ease, splendor, external prosperity, conquest had no part in its establishment. Other empires have been founded in the blood of the vanquished. The dominion of Christ was founded in His own blood. Most of the beatitudes which He pronounced in His infinite compassion have the sorrows of the earth for their subject but the joys of heaven for their completion.

To establish this religion in the world the Almighty, as His own Word assures us, subverted kingdoms and altered the face of nations. "For thus saith the Lord of Hosts," says Haggai, "yet once, it is a little while, and I will shake the heavens and the earth, and the sea and the dry land; and I will shake all nations and the Desire of all nations shall come." (Hag. 2:6,7a) Could a religion, the kingdom of which was to be founded by such awful means, be established and perpetuated without involving the sufferings of its subjects?

If the Christian life had been meant to be a path of roses, would the life of the Author of Christianity have been a path strewn with thorns? "He made for us," says Jeremy Taylor, "a covenant of sufferings; His very promises were sufferings, His rewards were sufferings, and His arguments to invite men to follow Him were only taken from sufferings in this life and the reward [for these] sufferings hereafter."

No prince but the Prince of Peace ever set out with a proclamation of the future nature of his empire. No other king desiring to allay avarice and check ambition ever invited his subjects by the unattractive declaration that his "kingdom was not of this world." (Jn. 18:36) No other sovereign ever declared that it was not dignity or honors, valor or talents that made them worthy of him, but it is their "taking up the cross" (Matt. 16:24) that brings them close to Him. If no other lord ever made the sorrows which would attend his followers a motive for their allegiance, we must remember that no other ever had the goodness to promise or the power to make good His promise that He would give rest to "the heavy laden." (Matt. 11:28) Other kings have overcome the world for their own ambition, but none other ever made the suffering involved in achieving that conquest a ground for motivating his followers to faithfulness.

In his letter to the Philippians, Paul enumerates the honors and distinctions prepared for his most favored converts, that they should not only believe in Christ, but that they should also suffer for him. Any other religion would use such a promise to deter, not to attract potential converts. That a religion should flourish under such discouraging invitations, with the threat of degrading circumstances and absolute losses, is unanswerable evidence that our faith was not of human origin.

It is among the mercies of God that he strengthens servants by hardening them through adverse circumstances, instead of leaving them to languish under the shining but withering sun of unclouded prosperity. When they cannot be attracted to Him by gentler influences, He sends these storms and tempests which purify while they alarm. Our gracious Father knows how long the happiness of eternity will be for His children.

The character of Christianity may be seen by how often the Scriptures use the image of military conflict to illustrate it. Suffering is the initiation into a Christian's calling. It is our education for heaven. Shall the scholar rebel at the discipline which is to fit him for his profession, or the soldier at the exercise which is to qualify him for victory?

But our trials do not all spring from outside ourselves. We would think them comparatively easy if we had only the opposition of men to struggle against, or even the severer measures of God to sustain. If we have a conflict with the world, we have a harder conflict within ourselves. Our bosom foe is our most unyielding enemy.

This is what makes our other trials heavy, which makes our power for enduring them weak, which renders our conquest over them slow and inconclusive.

This world is the stage on which worldly men act. The things of the world and the applause of the world are the rewards which they propose for themselves. These they often attain, and are thereby satisfied. They aim at no higher end. But let us not long for the success of those whose motives we reject, whose practices we dare not adopt, whose end we deplore. If we feel any inclination to murmur when we see the worldly in great prosperity, let us ask ourselves if we would tread their path to attain their end, if we would do their work to obtain their wages. We know that we would not. Let us then cheerfully leave them to scramble for the prizes and jostle for the places which the world temptingly holds out, but which we will not purchase at the world's price.

Good causes are not always conducted by good men. A good cause may be connected with something that is not good. The right cause is promoted and effected by some lesser, or even unworthy one. Whereas worldly people may be suspicious of a cause espoused by Christians, the support of influential persons outside the Church can well erase their suspicions. The character of the lofty cause may perhaps have to be lowered to suit the general taste, even to obtain the acceptance of the people for whose benefit it is intended.

We still fall into the error of which the prophet so long ago complained: "We call the proud happy" (Mal. 3:15) and the wicked fortunate. We may find ourselves envious of the powerful and influential. We feel this way, even when we remember that after the person has finished the work, the divine Employer throws that person aside, cut off and left to perish.

But you envy the powerful in the meantime, even though they have sacrificed every principle of justice, truth and mercy. Is this a man to be envied? Is this a prosperity to be coveted? Would you incur the penalties of that happiness?

But is it happiness to commit sin, to be abhorred by the upright in character, to offend God, and to ruin one's own soul? Do you really consider a temporary success compensation enough for deeds which will insure eternal misery to the doer? *Is* the successful bad person happy? Of what materials then is happiness made? Is it composed of a disturbed mind and an unquiet conscience? Are doubt and difficulty, are terror and apprehension, are distrust and suspicion, the gratification for which Christians would renounce their peace, displease their Maker, and would risk their soul? Think of the hidden vulture that feeds on the hearts of successful wickedness, and your longings and envy will cease. Your indignation will be changed into compassion, your denunciations into prayer.

But if such a person feels neither the scourge of conscience nor the sting of remorse, pity that individual the more. Pity them for the very want of that addition to their unhappiness, for if they added to their miseries the anticipation of their punishment, they might be led by repentance to avoid it. Can you reckon the blinding of their eyes and the hardening of their heart any part of their happiness? This opinion, however, is being expressed whenever we grudge the prosperity of the wicked. God, by delaying the punishment of bad people may have designs of mercy of which we know nothing— mercy perhaps to them, or if not to them, yet mercy to those who are suffering because of their actions, whom He intends through these bad instruments, to punish, and by punishing, eventually to save.

There is a sentiment even more bizarre than envy which prosperous wickedness excites in certain minds, and that is respect; but this feeling is never raised unless both the wickedness and the prosperity be on a grand scale. This sentiment exposes the belief that God does not govern human affairs, or that our motives do not concern Him, or that prosperity is a certain proof of His favor.

But though God may be patient with triumphant wickedness, He does not wink at or connive with it. The difference between being permitted and being supported, between being employed and approved, is greater than we are ready to acknowledge. Perhaps "the iniquity of the Amorites is not yet full." (Gen. 15:16) God has always the means of punishment as well as of pardon in His own hands. However, for God to punish at the exact moment when we demand it, might abort His greater plan and diminish the larger consequences. "They have drunk their hemlock," says a fine writer, "but the poison does not yet work." Let us not be impatient to administer a sentence which infinite justice sees right to defer. Let us think more of restraining our own vindictive tempers than of precipitating their destruction. They may yet repent of the crimes they are perpetrating. By some scheme, intricate and unintelligible to us, God may still pardon the sin which we think exceeds the limits even of His mercy.

We contrive to make revenge itself look like religion. We call down thunder on many a head under the pretence that those on whom we invoke it are God's enemies, when perhaps we invoke it because they are ours.

Though they should go on fully prosperous to the end, will it not cure our impatience to know that their end must come? Will it not satisfy us that they must die, that they must come to judgment? Which is to be envied, the Christian who dies ending their brief sorrows, or the one who closes a prosperous life and enters on a miserable eternity? The first has nothing to fear if the promises of the Gospel be true, the other has nothing to hope for, if they are factual. The Word of God must be a lie, heaven a fable, hell an invention, before the impenitent sinner can be safe. Is that person to be envied whose security depends on their falsehood? Is the other to be pitied whose hope is founded on their reality?

In estimating the comparative happiness of good and bad people, we should ever bear in mind that of all the calamities which can be inflicted or suffered, sin is the greatest; and of all punishments, insensibility to sin is the heaviest which the wrath of God inflicts in this world. God lets the wicked continue their smooth and prosperous course to the awful destiny in store for them, which will only be revealed when there is no longer any room for mercy.

We can see this same truth without looking to the hereafter and consulting only the present suffering. If we put the inward consolation derived from communion with God, the humble confidence of prayer, the devout trust in divine protection on the scale opposite to all the unjust power ever bestowed or guilty wealth ever possessed, we shall have no hesitation in deciding on which side even present happiness lies.

With a mind thus fixed, with a faith thus firm, one great object so absorbs the Christian that our peace is not tossed about by the things which confuse ordinary people. The Christian afflicted in the world may say, "My fortune is shattered; but since I made not gold my confidence while I possessed it, in losing it I have not lost myself. I leaned not on power, for I knew its instability. Had prosperity been my dependence, I would have fallen when it was removed."

Many lament the Christian who suffers while innocent. Surely believers should not try to avoid suffering by sinful conformity to worldly standards! Think how ease would be destroyed by the price paid for it! How short a time he would enjoy it, even if it were not bought at the expense of his soul!

Because of the benefits that suffering brings to the Christian's character, we can say that suffering itself is the reward of virtue. It becomes not only the instrument of promoting virtue, but the instrument of rewarding it. Besides, God promises a future reward to his children who suffer. To suppose that He *cannot* ultimately compensate His virtuous afflicted children is to believe Him less powerful than an earthly father—to suppose that He *will* not, is to believe Him less merciful.

Great trials are more often proofs of favor than of displeasure. An inferior officer will suffice for inferior expeditions, but the Sovereign selects the ablest general for the most difficult service. And not only does the King evidence his favor by the selection, but the soldier proves his attachment by rejoicing in the preference. One victory gained is no reason for his being set aside. One conquest only qualifies him for new attacks, suggests a reason for his being again employed.

The sufferings of good men by no means contradict the promise "that the meek shall inherit the earth." (Matt. 5:5) They "possess" it in such a way that they are willing to give it up when called to do so.

The belief that trials will facilitate salvation is another source of consolation. Sufferings also diminish the dread of death by cheapening the price of life. The affections even of the devout Christian are too much drawn downwards. Our heart too fondly cleaves to the dust, though we know that only trouble can spring from it. How would it be if we invariably possessed present enjoyments, and if a long panorama of delights lay always open before us? We have a far greater comfort in our own honest consciousness. Our Christian feelings under trials are a cheering evidence that our devotion is sincere. The gold has been melted down, and its purity is ascertained.

Among our other advantages, the afflicted Christian can apply to the mercy of God, but not as a new and uncertain resource. We do not come as an alien before a strange master, but as a child into the well-known presence of a tender father. We did not use prayer as a *final resort* to be used only in the great water floods. We had long and diligently sought God in the calm; we had clung to him, before we were driven to Him. We had sought God's favor while we still enjoyed the favor of the world. We did not defer our meditations on heavenly things to the disconsolate hour when earth had nothing for us. We can cheerfully associate our faith with those former days of felicity, when, with everything before us out of which to choose, we chose God. We not only feel the support derived from our present prayers, but the benefit of all those which we offered up in the day of joy and gladness. We will especially derive comfort from the supplications we had made for the anticipated though unknown trial of the present hour, and which in such a world of change it was reasonable to expect.

Let us confess then, that in all the trying circumstances of this changeful scene there is something infinitely soothing to the feelings of a Christian and inexpressibly tranquillizing to our mind to know that we have nothing to do with events but to submit to them. We have nothing to do with the revolutions of life but to acquiesce in them as the offerings of eternal wisdom. We do not need to take the management out of the hands of Providence, but submissively to follow the divine leading. We do not have to scheme for tomorrow, but to live in the present with cheerful resignation. Let us be thankful that as we can not by foreseeing prevent them, we can be thankful for ignorance where knowledge would only prolong and not prevent our suffering. We have grace which has promised that our strength shall be proportioned to our day. By the goodness of God these trials may be used for the noblest purposes. The quiet acquiescence of the heart and the submission of the will under actual trials, great or small, are more acceptable to God and more indicative of true faith, than the strongest general resolutions of firm action and deep submission under the most trying of imagined events. In the latter case it is the imagination which submits: in the former case it is the will.

We are too ready to imagine that there is no other way to serve God but by active exertions; exertions which only indulge our natural appetite, and gratify our own inclinations. It is an error to imagine that God who puts us into different situations, puts it out of our power to glorify him. Every circumstance may be turned to some good, either for ourselves or for others. Joseph in his prison under the strongest restrictions, loss of liberty, and a shattered reputation, made way for both his own high advancement and for the deliverance of Israel. Daniel in his dungeon, not only the destined prey, but in the very jaws of furious beasts, converted the king of Babylon and brought him to the knowledge of the true God. Could prosperity have achieved the former? Would not prosperity have prevented the latter?

We may often wonder why many of God's servants who are eminently fitted to instruct and reform the people of the land are disqualified by disease and thereby set aside from their public duty of which the necessity is so obvious and the fruits so remarkable. It may also cause us concern that many others possess uninterrupted health and strength, who are little gifted and at that, not even motivated to assist the welfare of the world in which they live.

But God's ways are not as our ways. He is not accountable to His creatures. The questioner needs to know why it is right. The suffering Christian believes and feels it to be right, humbly acknowledging the necessity of the affliction which friends are lamenting. This believer feels the mercy of what others are seeing as injustice. With deep humility this one is persuaded that if the affliction is not yet withdrawn, it is because it has not yet accomplished the purpose for which it was sent. The deprivation is probably intended both for the individual interests of the sufferer and for the reproof of those who have neglected to profit by this believer's labors. Perhaps God especially draws still nearer to Himself the one who had drawn so many others.

We are too ready to consider suffering as an indication of God's displeasure, not so much against sin in general as against the individual sufferer. Were this the case then those saints and martyrs who have pined in exile and groaned in dungeons and expired on scaffolds would have been the objects of God's peculiar wrath instead of His favor. But the truth is that our unbelief enters into almost all our reasoning on these topics. We do not constantly take into account a future state. We want God, if I may hazard the expression, to justify Himself as He goes. We cannot give Him even such long credit as the length of a human life. He must every moment be vindicating His character against every skeptical critic. He must unravel His plans to every shallow judge, revealing the knowledge of His design before its operations are completed. If we may adopt a phrase from a more common use, we will trust Him no farther than we can see Him. Though He has said, "Judge nothing before the time," we judge instantly, and therefore rashly, and in a word falsely. We would have more patience with God if we kept the brevity of earthly prosperity and suffering, the certainty of God's justice, and the eternity of future blessedness perpetually in view.

Even in judging fiction we are more just. During the

reading of a tragedy, though we feel for the distresses of those involved, yet we do not form an ultimate judgment of the propriety or injustice of their sufferings until the end. We give the poet credit either that they will extricate them from their distresses, or eventually explain the justice of them. We do not condemn them at the end of every scene for the trials which the sufferers do not appear to have deserved, nor for the sufferings which do not always seem to have arisen from their own misconduct. We behold the trials of the virtuous with sympathy and the successes of the wicked with indignation, but we do not pass our final sentence till the poet has passed his. We reserve our decisive judgment till the last scene closes and till the curtain drops. Shall we not treat the schemes of infinite Wisdom with as much respect as the plot of a drama?

If we might borrow an illustration from the legal profession, in a court of justice the bystanders do not give their sentence in the midst of a trial. We wait patiently till all the evidence is collected, carefully detailed and finally summed up. We then commonly applaud the justice of the jury and the equity of the judge, even though human decisions are imperfect and fallible. The felon they condemn, we rarely acquit; where they release the accused, we rarely denounce it. It is only *infinite Wisdom* on whose purposes we cannot rely; it is only *infinite Mercy* whose operations we cannot trust. It is only "the Judge of all the earth" who cannot do right. We reverse the order of God by summoning *Him* to our bar, at whose awful bar we shall soon be judged.

But to return to our more immediate point: the apparently unfair distribution of prosperity between good and bad people. While the good constantly derive their happiness from a sense of God's omniscience, the other finds it frightful. The eye of God is a pillar of light to the one, and a cloud of darkness to the other. The awful thought, *"Thou, God, seest all!"* is as much a terror to persons who dread His justice as it is a joy to those who derive all their support from it.

The one who may feel sad, is safe, while the other, though confident, is insecure. He is as far from peace as he is from God. Every day brings Christians nearer to their crown; sinners are every day working their way nearer to their ruin. The hour of death, which the one dreads as something worse than extinction, is to the other the hour of nativity, the birthday of immortality. At the height of his sufferings the good person knows that he will soon die. At the zenith of his success the sinner has a similar assurance, but how different is the result of the same conviction! An invincible faith sustains the one in the severest straits, while an unavoidable dread gives the lie to the proudest triumphs of the other.

The only happy person, after all, is not the one whom worldly prosperity renders apparently happy, but the one who no change of worldly circumstances can make essentially miserable. The latter's peace does not depend on external events, but on an internal support; not on that success which is common to all, but on that hope which is his peculiar privilege. It rests on that promise which is the sole prerogative of the Christian.

Chapter 19
Facing Sickness and Death

The pagan philosophers have given many admirable precepts for enduring misfortunes; but lacking the motives and supports of the Christian faith, though they excite much intellectual admiration, they produce little practical results. The stars which glittered in their moral night, though bright, imparted no warmth. Their dissertations on death had no charm to extract death's sting. We receive no support from their elaborate treatises on immortality because they did not know Him who "brought life and immortality to light." (II Tim. 1:10) Their consolations could not strip the grave of its terrors, for to them it was not "swallowed up in victory." (I Cor. 15:54) To conceive of the soul as an immortal principle, without the pardon of its sins, was but cold comfort. Their future state was but a happy guess; their heaven but a conjecture.

When we read their compositions, we admire the manner in which the medicine is administered, but we do not find it effectual for the cure. The beauty of the sentiment we applaud, but our heart continues to ache. There is no healing balm in their elegant prescription. These four little words, *"Thy will be done,"* contain a remedy of more powerful efficacy than all the discipline of the Stoic school.

What sufferer ever derived any ease from the observation, that "pain is very troublesome, but I am resolved never to acknowledge it to be an evil"? He does not directly say that pain is not an evil, but by a sophistical turn professes that philosophy will never confess it to be an evil. But what consolation does the sufferer draw from the quibbling nicety? "What difference is there," as Archbishop Tillotson well inquires, "between things being troublesome and being evil, when all the evil of an affliction lies in the trouble it creates to us?"

Christianity knows none of these fanciful distinctions. She never pretends to insist that pain is not an evil, but she does more; she converts it into a good. Christianity therefore teaches a fortitude more noble than philosophy; just as meeting pain with resignation to the hand that inflicts it, is more heroic than denying it to be an evil.

To submit on the mere human ground that there is no alternative, is not resignation but hopelessness. To bear affliction solely because impatience will not remove it may be a just reason for bearing it, but it is an inferior one. It savors rather of despair than submission when not sanctioned by a higher principle. "It is the Lord, let Him do what seemeth to Him good," (I Sam. 3:18) is at once a motive of more powerful obligation than all the documents which philosophy ever suggested; a firmer ground of support than all the energies that natural strength ever supplied.

Under any visitation, sickness for instance, God permits us to think the affliction "not joyous but grievous." (Heb. 12:11) But though He allows us to feel dejected, we must not allow ourselves to be so. There is again a sort of heroism in bearing up against affliction, which some adopt on the ground that it raises their character and confers dignity on their suffering. This philosophic firmness is far from being the attitude which Christianity inspires.

When we are compelled by the Hand of God to endure sufferings, we must not endure them on the poor principle that they are inevitable. We must not, with a sullen courage, collect ourselves into a center of our own; into a cold apathy to everything else and a proud praise of all within. We must not concentrate our scattered faults into a sort of dignified selfishness nor adopt an independent correctness. A gloomy Stoicism is not Christian heroism. A melancholy passivity is not Christian resignation.

Nor must we compensate ourselves for our outward self-control by secret murmurings. It is inward discontent that we must endeavor to repress. It is the discontent of the heart, the unexpressed but not unfelt murmur, against which we must pray for grace and struggle for resistance. We must not smother our discontents before others, and feed on them in private. It is the hidden rebellion of the will we must subdue, if we would submit as Christians. Nor must we justify our impatience by saying that if our affliction did not disqualify us from being useful to our families and active in the service of God, we could bear it more cheerfully. Let us rather be assured that our suffering does not disqualify us for that duty which we most need, and to which God calls us by that very suffering.

A constant posture of defense against the attacks of our great spiritual enemy is a better security than an occassional blow or victory. It is also a better preparation for all the occurrences of life. It is not some notable act of mortification, but an habitual state of discipline which will prepare us for great trials. A soul ever on the watch, fervent in prayer, diligent in self-inspection, frequent in meditation, fortified against the vanities of time by repeated views of eternity will be better able to resist temptation.

"Strong in the Lord and in the power of His might," (Eph. 6:10) the heart will be enabled to resist temptation and expel the tempter. To a mind so prepared, the thoughts of sickness will not be new, for it knows it is the "condition of the battle." The prospect of death will not be surprising, for he knows it is its termination.

When we face serious illness and the prospect of death, we must summon all the fortitude and all the resignation of the Christian. The principles we have been learning must now be made practical. The speculations we have admired must now become reality. All that we have been studying was in order to furnish materials for this great need. All the strength we have been collecting must now be brought into action. We must now draw to a point all the scattered arguments, all the different motives, and all the cheering promises of faith. We must exemplify all the rules we have given to others. We must embody all the resolutions we have formed for ourselves. We must reduce our precepts to experience. We must pass from discourses on submission to its exercise; from dissertations on suffering to enduring it. We must heroically call up the determinations of our better days. We must recollect what we have said about the support of faith and hope when our strength was in full vigor, when our heart was at ease, and our mind undisturbed. Let us collect all that remains to us of mental strength. Let us implore the aid of holy hope and fervent faith, to show that Christian commitment is not a beautiful theory but a soul-sustaining truth.

The strongest faith is needed in the hardest trials. To the confirmed Christian the highest degree of grace is commonly imparted during those trials. Do not injure that faith on which you rested when your mind was strong by suspecting its validity now that it is weak. That which had your full assent in perfect health, which was then firmly rooted in your spirit and grounded in your understanding, must not be damaged by the doubts of a weakened reason and the misgivings of an impaired judgment. You may not now be able to reason clearly, but you may derive strong consolation from conclusions which were once fully established in your mind.

The reflecting Christian will consider the natural evil of sickness as the consequence and punishment of moral evil. We will mourn, not only that we suffer pain, but because that pain is the effect of sin. If our race had not sinned we would not have suffered. The heaviest aggravation of our pain is to know that we have deserved it. But it is a counterbalance to this trial to know that our merciful Father has no pleasure in the sufferings of His children; that He chastens them in love; that He never inflicts a stroke which He could safely spare; that He inflicts it to purify as well as to punish, to caution as well as to cure.

What a support in the dreary season of sickness it is to reflect that the Captain of our salvation was made perfect through sufferings! What a comfort to remember that if we suffer with Him we shall also reign with Him! This implies also the reverse, that if we do not suffer with Him— that is, if we suffer merely because we cannot help it, without reference to Him, without suffering for His sake and in His Spirit, we shall not reign with Him. If it is not sanctified suffering it will avail but little. We shall not be paid for having suffered, as too many people believe, but our fitness for the kingdom of glory will be increased if we suffer according to His will and after His example.

Those who are brought to serious reflection by the salutary affliction of a sick bed, will look back with astonishment on their former false estimate of worldly things. Riches! Beauty! Pleasure! Genius! Fame! What are they in the eyes of the sick and dying?

Riches! These are so far from affording them a moment's ease, that it will be well if no remembrance of their misuse aggravate their present pains. They feel as if they only wished to live that they might henceforth dedicate their riches to the purposes for which they were given.

Beauty! What is beauty? they cry, as they consider their own sunken eyes, hollow cheeks, and pallid countenance. They acknowledge with the Psalmist that "Thou with rebukes dost correct man for iniquity, Thou makest his beauty to consume away like a moth." (Ps. 39:11)

Genius! What is it? Without faith, genius is only a lamp on the gate of a palace. It may serve to cast a gleam of light on those outside, but the inhabitant sits in darkness.

Pleasure! That has not left a trace behind it. It died in the birth, and is not therefore worthy to come into this bill of mortality.

Fame! Of this their very soul acknowledges the emptiness. They are astonished that they could ever have been so infatuated as to run after a sound, to pursue a shadow, to embrace a cloud. Augustus asked his friends as they surrounded his dying bed, if he had acted his part well. When they answered in the affirmative, he cried, "Applaud!" But the acclamations of the whole universe would mock rather than soothe the dying Christian if unsupported by the hope of God's approval. They now rate at its true value the fame which was so often eclipsed by envy, and which will be so soon forgotten in death. They have no ambition left but for heaven, where there will be neither envy, death, nor forgetfulness.

When capable of reflection, the sick Christian will go over the sins and errors of his past life, humbling himself for them as sincerely as if he had never repented of them before, imploring forgiveness as fervently as if he did not believe they were long since forgiven. The remembrance of our former offenses will grieve us, but the humble hope that they are pardoned will fill us "with joy unspeakable and full of glory."

Even in this state of helplessness we may improve our self-acquaintance. We may detect new deficiencies in our character, fresh imperfections in our virtues. Omissions will now strike us with the force of actual sins. Resignation, which we fancied was so easy when only the sufferings of others required it, we now find to be difficult when called on to practice it ourselves. We may have sometimes wondered at their impatience; we are now humbled at our own. We will not only try to bear patiently the pains we actually suffer, but will recollect gratefully those from which we have been delivered, and which we may have formerly found less bearable than our present sufferings.

In the extremity of pain we feel there is no consolation but in humble acquiescence in God's will. It may be that we can pray but little, but that little will be fervent. We can articulate perhaps not at all, but our prayer is addressed to One who sees the heart, who can interpret its language, who requires not words but love. A pang endured without a murmur, or only such an involuntary groan as nature compels and faith regrets, is itself a prayer.

If surrounded with all the accommodations of affluence, let us compare our own situation with that of thousands, who probably with greater merit and under more severe trials have not one of our means of relief. When invited to take a distasteful remedy, let us reflect how many perishing fellow creatures may be pining for that remedy, suffering additional distress from their inability to procure it.

In the lulls between bouts of severe pain we can turn our few advantages to the best account. We can make the most of every short respite, patiently bearing with little disappointments, little delays, with the awkwardness or accidental neglect of our attendants. Thankful for general kindness, we can accept good will instead of perfection. The suffering Christian will be grateful for small reliefs, little alleviations, short snatches of rest. Abated pain will be positive pleasure. The freer use of limbs which had nearly lost their activity, will be enjoyments.

The sufferer has perhaps often regretted that one of the worst effects of sickness is the selfishness it too naturally induces. We can resist the temptation to this by not being exacting and unreasonable in our requirements. Through our tenderness to the feelings of others, we can be careful not to add to their distress by any appearance of discontent.

What a lesson against selfishness have we in the conduct of our dying Redeemer! It was while bearing His cross to the place of execution that He said to the sorrowing multitude, "Weep not for me, but for yourselves and for your children." While enduring the agonies of crucifixion He endeavored to mitigate the sorrows of His mother and of His friend by tenderly committing them to each other's care. While sustaining the pangs of death, He gave the immediate promise of heaven to the expiring criminal.

Christians should review, if able, not only the sins, but the mercies of our past life. If we were previously accustomed to unbroken health, we can bless God for the long period in which we have enjoyed it. If continued infirmity has been our portion, we will feel grateful that we have had such a long and gradual weaning from the world. From either state we can derive consolation. If the pain is new, what a mercy to have hitherto escaped it! If habitual, we bear more easily what we have borne long.

We can also review our temporal blessings and deliverances, our domestic comforts, our Christian friendships. Among other mercies, our now "purged eyes" will add up our difficulties, our sorrows and trials and find a new and heavenly light thrown on that passage "It is good for me that I have been afflicted." (Ps. 119:71) It seems to us as if hitherto, we had only heard it with the hearing of our ears, but now our eyes see it. If we are real Christians, and have had enemies, we will always have prayed for them, but now we will be thankful for them. We will the more earnestly implore mercy for them as instruments which have helped to fit us for our present state. He will look up with holy gratitude to the great Physician, who by a kind of "divine chemistry" in making up events, has made that one unpalatable ingredient, at the bitterness of which we once revolted, the very means by which all other things have worked together for good; had they worked separately they would not have worked efficaciously.

Under the most severe visitation, let us compare our own sufferings with the cup which our Redeemer drank for our sakes. Let us compare our condition with that of the Son of God. He was deserted in His most trying hour; deserted probably by those whose limbs, sight and life He had restored, whose souls He had come to save. We are surrounded by unwearied friends; every pain is mitigated by sympathy, every want not only relieved but prevented. When our souls are "exceeding sorrowful," our friends participate in our sorrow; when desired "to watch" with us, they watch not "one hour" but many, not falling asleep, not forsaking us in our "agony" but sympathizing where they cannot relieve.

Besides this, we must acknowledge with the penitent malefactor, "We indeed suffer justly but this man hath done nothing amiss." (Lk. 23:41) We suffer for our offenses the inevitable penalty of our fallen nature. He bore our sins and those of the whole human race.

How cheering in this forlorn state to reflect that He not only suffered for us then, but is sympathizing with us now; that "in all our afflictions He is afflicted." (Isa. 63:9) The tenderness of His sympathy seems to add a value to our sacrifice, while the severity of our suffering makes His sympathy more dear to us.

If our intellectual powers be mercifully preserved, how

many virtues may now be brought into exercise which
had either lain dormant or been considered as of inferior
worth in the prosperous day of activity. The Christian
disposition indeed seems to be more evident and to be
exercised more vigorously on a sick bed. The passive
virtues, the least brilliant but the most difficult, are then
particularly called into action. To suffer the whole will
of God on the tedious bed of suffering is often more trying
than to perform the most shining exploit on the stage
of the world. The hero in the field of battle has the love
of fame as well as patriotism to support him. He knows
that the witnesses of his valor will be the heralds of his
renown. The martyr at the stake is divinely strengthened.
Extraordinary grace is imparted for extraordinary trials.
The martyr's pangs are exquisite but they are short. The
crown is in sight; it is almost in possession. By faith, Stephen
said, "I see the heavens opened, and the Son of man
standing on the right hand of God." (Acts 7:56) But to
be strong in faith and patient in hope in a long and
lingering sickness is an example of more general use and
ordinary application, than the sublime heroism of the
martyr. We read of the martyr with astonishment. Our
faith is strengthened, and our admiration kindled. But we
read it without that peculiar reference to our own
circumstances which we feel in cases that are likely to
apply to ourselves. With a dying friend we have not only
a feeling of tenderness, but there is also a community
of interests. The certain conviction that his case must soon
be our own, makes it our own now. To the martyr's stake
we feel that we are not likely to be brought. To the dying
bed we must inevitably come.

Accommodating our state of mind to the nature of
our disease, the dying Christian will derive consolation
in any case, either from thinking how forcibly a sudden
sickness breaks the chain which binds us to the world,
or how gently a gradual decay unties it. We will feel and

acknowledge the necessity of all we suffer to wean us from life. We admire the divine goodness which commissions the infirmities of sickness to divest the world of its enchantments and to strip death of some of its most formidable terrors. We feel much less reluctant to leave a body exhausted by suffering rather than one in the vigor of health.

Sickness, instead of narrowing the heart in self-centeredness, which is its worst effect on a carnal mind, enlarges the Christian's heart. We earnestly exhort those around us to defer no act of repentance, no labor of love, no deed of justice, no work of mercy, because of the sickness in which we now lie.

How many motives has the Christian to restrain his murmurs! Murmuring offends God because it injures His goodness and because it perverts the occasion which God has now afforded for giving an opportunity to display an example of patience. Let us not complain that we have nothing to do in sickness when we are furnished with the *opportunity* and called to the *duty* of resignation. The duty indeed is always ours, but the occasion is now more prominently given. Let us not say even in this depressed state that we have nothing to be thankful for. If sleep be afforded, let us acknowledge the blessing. If wearisome nights be our portion, let us remember they are "appointed to us." Let us mitigate the grievance of watchfulness by considering it as a sort of prolongation of life; as the gift of more minutes granted for meditation and prayer. If we are not able to employ it to either of these purposes, there is a fresh occasion for exercising that resignation which will be accepted for both.

If reason be continued, yet with sufferings too intense for any spiritual duty, the sick Christian may take comfort that the business of life was accomplished before the sickness began. We will not be terrified if duties are superseded, for we have nothing to do but to die. This is the act for which all other acts, all other duties, and all other means, have been preparing us. They who have long been accustomed to look death in the face, and who have often anticipated the agonies of their deteriorating nature, and who have accustomed themselves to pray for support under them, will now feel the blessed effect of those petitions which have long been treasured in heaven. To those very anticipatory prayers we may now owe the humble confidence of hope in this inevitable hour. Accustomed to contemplation, we will not, at least, have the dreadful addition of surprise and novelty to aggravate the trying situation. It has long been familiar to our mind, though beforehand it could only exist as a faint picture compared to a reality. Faith will not so much dwell on the open grave as look forward to the glories to which it leads. The hope of heaven will soften the pangs which lie in the way to it. On heaven we can fix our eyes rather than on the fearful intervening circumstances. We will not dwell on the struggle which is for a moment, but on the crown which is for ever. We will endeavor to think less of death than of its Conqueror, less of the grave than its Spoiler, less of the body in ruins than of the spirit in glory, less of the darkness of our closing day than of the opening dawn of immortality. In some brighter moments, when viewing our eternal redemption drawing nigh, we may exclaim, "Our soul is escaped as a bird out of the snare of the fowlers: the snare is broken, and we are escaped." (Ps. 124:7)

If we ever wish for recovery, it is in order to glorify God by our future life more than we have done in the past. But as we know the deceitfulness of our heart, we are not certain that this would be the case. Yet should we be restored, we humbly resolve in a better strength than our own, to dedicate our life to the Restorer.

When death nears, our prospects as to this world are at an end also. We commit ourselves unreservedly to our heavenly Father. But though secure in our destination, we may still dread the passage. The Christian will rejoice that our rest is at hand, though we may shudder at the unknown transit. Though faith is strong, nature may be weak. Nay in this awful crisis strong faith is sometimes rendered faint through the weakness of nature.

At the moment when our faith is looking round for every additional confirmation, we may rejoice in those blessed certainties, those glorious realizations which Scripture affords. We may take comfort that the strongest witnesses given by the apostles to the reality of the heavenly state were not mere speculation. They spake what they knew and testified what they had seen. "I reckon," says St Paul, "that the sufferings of this present time are not worthy to be compared with the glory which shall be revealed in us." (Rom. 8:18) He said this after he had been caught up into the third heaven, and after he had beheld the glories to which he alludes. The author of the Book of Revelation, having described the indescrible glories of the new Jerusalem, thus puts new life and power into his description: "I John *saw* these things, and heard them." (Rev. 22:8)

The power to distinguish objects increases as they grow nearer. Christians feel that they are entering a state where every care will cease, every fear vanish, every desire be fulfilled, every sin be done away, and every grace perfected. There will be no more temptations to resist, no more passions to subdue, no more insensibility to mercies, no more deadness in service, no more wandering in prayer, no more sorrows to be felt for themselves, nor tears to be shed for others. They are going where their devotion will be without apathy, their love without alloy; their doubts will turn to certainty, their expectation to enjoyment, and their hope to fruition. All will be perfect, for God will be all in all.

We know that we shall derive all our happiness immediately from God. It will no longer pass through any of those channels which now sully its purity. It will be offered us through no second cause which may fail, no intermediate agent which may deceive, no uncertain medium which may disappoint. The bliss is not only certain, but perfect—not only perfect, but eternal.

As we approach the land of realities, the shadows of this earth cease to interest or mislead us. The films are removed from our eyes. Objects are stripped of their false luster. Nothing that is really little any longer looks great. The mists of vanity are dispersed. Everything which is to have an end appears small, appears nothing. Eternal things assume their proper magnitude—for we behold them with a true vision. We have ceased to lean on the world for we have found it both a reed and a spear. It has failed and it has pierced us. We lean not on ourselves, for we have long known our own weakness. We lean not on our virtues, for they can do nothing for us. If we had no better refuge in death, we feel that our sun would set in darkness and our love close in despair.

But we know in whom we have trusted. We look upward with holy but humble confidence to that Great Shepherd, who having long since led us into green pastures, having corrected us by His rod, and by His staff supported us, will, we humbly trust, guide us through the dark valley of the shadow of death, and safely land us on the peaceful shores of everlasting rest.

Printed by Paraclete Press
Orleans, MA　02653
1-800-451-5006